Wit as a Weapon

The Political Joke in History

Egon Larsen

Frederick Muller Limited
London

First published in Great Britain 1980 by
Frederick Muller Limited, London NW2 6LE

British Library Cataloguing in Publication Data

Larsen, Egon
   Wit as a weapon.
   1. Political satire
   I. Title
   809.7'9'35   PN6149.P64
   ISBN 0–584–10395–6

Typeset by Computacomp (UK) Ltd.,
Fort William, Scotland
Printed in Great Britain by Biddles Ltd., Guildford, Surrey

Contents

1

Jokes: The People's Voice

Ivan sits on the Kremlin wall, a trumpet beside him. Sergei, his friend, passes by and sees him up there.
'What's the idea, Ivan?'
'It's my new job. I'm waiting for the world revolution. When it comes I have to announce the good news by blowing my trumpet.'
'And how much do they pay you?'
'One rouble for each day I have to sit here.'
'That's very little, Ivan.'
'I know, Sergei. But it's a job for life.'

This story, which was widely told in Russia during the early years of the revolution, is typical of the political jokes which have been circulating throughout history in periods of stress and hardship, particularly in countries where authoritarian regimes suppressed freedom of speech. That joke, ridiculing the professed aims and expectations of the establishment, is also typical because it was told, and is still being told, in other countries and against other regimes – the Jacobins during the French Revolution, the Hitler regime, and now in eastern Europe, with variations but more or less the same punch-line.

Another recurrent story is that about the glass eye, which seems to have originated in colonial times in Africa or America when it took the form of a dialogue between master and slave. It turned up again in Nazi

Germany when the Gestapo was hunting down members of various religious groups, not only Jews but also Jehovah's Witnesses and anthroposophists. This was the version told among the latter sect:

'I will let you go free,' says the Gestapo man who is very proud of his well-made glass eye, 'if you can tell me which of my eyes is artificial.'

The anthroposophist replies without hesitation, 'The right one.'

'And how did you find out?'

'Very easily. That eye seems to show a trace of human feeling.'

Such jokes cannot, of course, originate in journals, newspapers or books in the countries concerned since there is no freedom of the press. As a rule, one cannot tell where they came from, who invented them and when or where they appeared for the first time. Their common denominator is that they pass from mouth to mouth among the 'silent majority', the people who have been deprived of legitimate means of expression. Thus jokes assume the role of the *vox populi* in countries and periods lacking free elections, a properly functioning parliament, satirical magazines and, in our time, uncensored radio and television.

Surprisingly, the phenomenon of the political joke has attracted little interest as a subject of serious research. The exception is Henri Bergson, the French philosopher, who wrote in his work *Le Rire* (1900) about the 'conspiratorial power of laughter, by which society avenges itself for the liberties taken with it ... The function of laughter is to intimidate by ridicule ... Laughter is always the laughter of a group; however spontaneous it seems, it always implies a kind of freemasonry, or even complicity, with other laughers, real or imaginary.'

Sigmund Freud, who wrote a whole volume on *Jokes and their Relation to the Unconscious* (1905) and later an essay on *Humour* (1927), does not analyze political jokes, though he deals extensively with what he calls 'tendentious' ones; here, he says, aggression is the motive force: 'Humour is not resigned, it is rebellious. It signifies not only the triumph of the ego but also of the pleasure principle, which is able to assert itself here against the unkindness of the real circumstances.'

The nearest Freud gets to an analysis of the political joke is this:

> By making our enemy small, inferior, despicable or comic, we achieve in a roundabout way the enjoyment of overcoming him ... A joke will allow us to exploit something ridiculous in our enemy which we could not, because of obstacles in our way, bring forward openly or consciously ... Tendentious jokes are especially favoured in order to make aggressiveness or criticism possible against persons in exalted positions who claim to exercise authority. The joke then represents a rebellion against that authority, a liberation from its pressure.

To some extent, of course, the political joke *is* a safety valve or, as some observers would say, a way in which an oppressed people preserves its sanity. Jokes may not be able to topple a dictatorial regime; but there is one important point which adds to the effectiveness of political humour: the oppressors have no defence against it. If they try to fight back they appear only more ridiculous. Furthermore, they cannot punish the perpetrator – unless they catch him, as it were, red-mouthed. Since anti-authoritarian jokes exist mainly in the ephemeral element of the spoken word – the Germans called them *Flüsterwitze*, whispered jokes, in the Nazi era – the angry rulers would hit only the empty air if they lashed out at them.

How do these jokes manage to get recorded for posterity? 'Underground' pamphlets or journals, produced secretly, use them; exiles from totalitarian countries and newspaper correspondents bring them to the outside world; or they survive the regimes they have

attacked, and are published when the political situation
has changed. Others, like the job-for-life or the glass-eye
stories, experience a series of reincarnations. However,
that chance of survival depends on the simplicity, and
thereby effectiveness, of a joke: involved stories, which
need much historical explanation, do not keep well, and
this may be the reason why so few political jokes have
come down to us from antiquity.

The ancient Greeks certainly had a strong sense of
humour, as we know from their comedies, especially
those by Aristophanes who lived around 400 BC, at the
time of the Peloponnesian War between Athens and
Sparta. It was also the time of the Athenian demagogue
Cleon. Aristophanes caricatured him in his comedies as
an unscrupulous warmonger, and Cleon hit back by
trying to deprive the dramatist of his civil rights. We may
assume that many more jokes about and against Cleon
were circulating among the Athenians, while the people
of Sparta made sarcastic quips about the austere life-style
imposed on them during the war. For instance, they were
forced to have their meals at public tables, with 'black
broth' as the main course – a kind of blood soup so
revolting that it was said Spartans preferred dying in
battle to living on black broth.
    It was also the period of some of Greece's great
philosophers, and there were a few popular stories about
their disregard for the high and mighty. Plato, it was said,
visited Syracuse, and the new local tyrant, Dionysius the
Younger, invited him for a symposium. 'What do they
say about me at the Athens Academy?' Dionysius asked
his guest. 'We have more important things to discuss
than you,' replied Plato. A classical anecdote about the
philosopher Diogenes, who was said to have made his
home in a tun, relates that he was once visited by
Alexander the Great who asked him whether there was
anything he could do for him. 'Yes,' said the philosopher,
'don't stand between me and the sun.'

The citizens of Rome hardly ever had any reason to express their political opinions in the form of whispered jokes; even the most autocratic of their rulers hesitated to ban public criticism. Caesar might have done so if he had survived as a dictator; but we know what happened to him. One story which circulated among the Romans when Caesar and Pompey were about to start their civil war, each of them securing financial backing and recruiting soldiers, was about a young man telling his friend that he has just signed on with Caesar's legions. 'You're doing the wrong thing,' said the friend. 'You should join Pompey – he's got more money.' 'Yes,' said the young man, 'but Caesar has more debts.' The implication was that Rome's capitalists had already invested a lot of money in Caesar's venture because they believed he would win against Pompey; and so he did.

We can only guess what the slaves, the proletariat of Roman society, thought about their masters; their revolts are recorded in history, but we know nothing about their jokes. On the other hand, some sayings of the rulers became very popular, though perhaps not in the way the speakers had intended. When the megalomaniac Emperor Nero died, all Rome laughed about his last words: 'What an artist dies in me!' Also proverbial became a wisecrack by the Emperor Vespasian. When his son Titus criticized him because of the introduction of a tax on public lavatories, Vespasian held the first coins collected by way of this system under Titus' nose with the words, '*Pecunia non olet*,' 'Money doesn't smell!'

For a thousand years after the fall of the Roman Empire the occidental world seems to have produced no political humour at all; whatever the common people may have thought or said about their temporal and clerical rulers has never been discovered, let alone recorded. It is only in the fourteenth century that we find signs of social rebellion. The prototype of all knavish fools, Till Eulenspiegel (or Ulenspiegel), was probably a historical

character of that period. Born in Brunswick, he roamed
Central Europe and Flanders. His dramatic adventures
and comical pranks were told by a great many people
and eventually published in the early sixteenth century.
He seems to have been active in the struggle of the
Flemings against their foreign oppressors – though not
against the Spaniards, as Charles de Coster, the
nineteenth-century Belgian poet, relates rather
anachronistically, for the Spanish occupation began only
two centuries after Ulenspiegel's death.

Ulenspiegel had an English equivalent called John
Scoggin (or Scogan), said to have been court fool to
Edward IV in the 1460s; his pranks were told among the
people with great relish and later collected in printed
books. Though Scoggin's practical jokes were often
aimed at the clergy, he was no political rebel, but wise
enough to keep on reasonable terms with his king and
queen.

One of the most famous slogans in the English
language is the text of a sermon which John Ball, priest
and insurgent, gave at the outbreak of the Peasants'
Revolt in 1381; it has come down to us in the form of this
two-liner:

> When Adam delved and Eve span,
> who was then the gentleman?

After the death of Wat Tyler, the peasants' leader, in the
battle of Smithfield, John Ball was captured and hanged
at St Albans.

Another cleric of the lower orders, William Langland –
probably in conjunction with some unknown co-authors
– wrote a famous Middle-English poem which offers
much insight into the lives and thoughts of the peasants
who rose in that bloody and tragic revolt: *The Vision of
Piers the Plowman*. Three versions, written between 1362
and 1398, have survived; it seems that the work became
very popular, with its fascinating mixture of allegory and
mysticism, primitive philosophy and homespun satire. It
was this last element of the poem which must have made

the downtrodden of medieval English society aware of their predicament; it denounced the corruption among the rich and the clergy, it castigated an inadequate government, it called the nation back to the simple virtues of a Christian life. The humour of *Piers Plowman* is often grim but hearty and effective.

Three major events, seemingly unconnected, brought the European Middle Ages to an end: the discovery of America, the invention of printing, and the Reformation. In fact, they were related by the crumbling of the influence which Roman Catholicism had wielded over the minds of the people, dictating what they should think and feel, and preventing any devlopment in science or philosophy which might challenge the Church's view of the world. Thus, Columbus' attempt at sailing westward to India was an act of rebellion; his journey proved that the earth was a globe and not a flat disc. The inevitable next step was to be the revelation that it was not the centre of the universe as the Church had been teaching, but just one of several planets revolving around the sun.

Already around 1450, forty years before the discovery of the New World beyond the Atlantic Ocean, the art and craft of printing with movable letters had been invented by a German artisan, Gutenberg, in Mainz (unless we accept the rival claim of a Dutch innkeeper, Laurens Coster of Haarlem). The art of printing spread quickly all over Europe, hastening the demise of the Dark Ages, liberating formidable forces of the human mind, and disseminating new ideas which attacked the powers of reaction, ignorance and intellectual oppression. Through the medium of the printed word, at least the educated could inform themselves of new theological concepts and geographical discoveries. Words in black on white penetrated the mental night in which the rulers of Europe wished to keep their subjects. Rebellious pamphlets and broadsheets prepared the greatest popular uprising in German history, the Peasants' Wars

of the early sixteenth century; and it was with Martin
Luther's treatises – especially *On the Liberty of a Christian
Man* (1520) – that the Reformation began.

Of course, the great majority of the common people
was still illiterate, but mouth-to-mouth jokes about the
Catholic establishment circulated in great numbers
before and during the Reformation. A very popular quip
of the late fifteenth century was: 'God is everywhere on
earth except in Rome – only His deputy is there.' There
was a story about the Medici Pope Leo X who organized a
general sale of indulgences to finance the building of St
Peter's Church in Rome – which prompted Luther to
publish his anti-indulgence *Resolutions*. Leo, the story
went, dies and goes to heaven, where he knocks on the
gate. St Peter calls out, 'Who's there?'

'It's me, the Pope. Open up!'

'But if you are the Pope, why don't you open the gate
yourself?' asks St Peter. 'Have you not got the keys to
heaven like all the popes before you?'

'I have the keys,' replies Leo, 'but Luther has changed
the lock.'

The resentment against the clerics was voiced in many
ways. In the Moselle region the peasants asked the jocular
question: 'Why has our river so many bends?' and the
answer was: 'There were such a lot of mendicant friars,
eating the food of the poor and growing so fat that the
Moselle had great trouble winding its way around them.'
In a similar vein, when a stroke of lightning hit the
outhouses of a monastery, the comment on the incident
was, 'The monks were lucky; if the kitchen had been
struck they'd all be dead!'

France abounded with anti-clerical jokes. A barren
lady, according to one of them, went to Chartres and told
a local woman that she had undertaken the pilgrimage in
the hope of being blessed with a child. 'Then you can
turn back straight away,' said the woman. 'The reverend
gentleman died yesterday.'

Amid the great religious upheaval, the Jews retained
their roles as the scapegoats and milch cows of the rulers.

A deputation from the Jews of Strasbourg, so one story goes, seeks an audience with the town's commandant.

'Throw them out,' he orders. 'These villains murdered our Lord and Saviour!'

'But sir,' says an officer, 'I hear they've brought a lot of money for the treasury.'

'Ah well,' grunts the commandant, 'let them in – after all, they didn't know what they were doing.'

·The people of Rome had their special place for political squibs, lampoons, and satirical hexameters: an ancient statue they had dug up in the fifteenth century, and which they called 'Pasquino' after a local tailor noted for his caustic wit. Anonymous wags inscribed on it their 'pasquinades' as the Pompeians had inscribed or scratched their *graffiti* on the walls. One famous pasquinade was a quip about Pope Innocent X, known for his immoral life and his liaison with the beautiful Roman courtesan Olympia. When he died, someone wrote on the Pasquino statue: 'Surely Innocent will go to heaven; he'll mount the Olympus all right, after mounting Olympia so many times in life!'

'Puritans' was at first a term of almost jocular derision in England, used for those extreme Protestants for whom the new Reformed Church was still riddled with 'popish' practices which they wished to eradicate. With the growth of their movement and its influence, Puritanism became a word for their general attitude to life, religious and secular. Their motto was 'The Bible, the whole Bible, and nothing but the Bible'; they demanded a high sense of duty and morality, rigorous personal devotion and an intense reforming zeal in human affairs. For many Englishmen the Puritan, strait-laced and opposed to the joys of life, was a figure of fun, like Malvolio in Shakespeare's *Twelfth Night*. The nineteenth-century historian Macaulay assumed that to the non-Puritans the sect appeared downright cranky and even mentally contorted. 'The Puritan,' he wrote, 'hated bearbaiting, not because it gave pain to the bear but because it gave pleasure to the spectators. Indeed he generally contrived

to enjoy the double pleasure of tormenting both
spectators and bear.'

When, under Cromwell, the Puritans did become the
dominant power in the land, one would have expected
them to be the targets of the people's sarcasm. But
strangely enough, the English suffered that joyless regime
– the nearest to a dictatorship the nation ever
experienced – with only some subdued murmurs of
opposition, leaving the fighting to the soldiers. Among
the few satirical attacks on the Lord Protector and the
Long Parliament was a series of single-sheet parodies of
religious texts, published (of course anonymously) in
1647. One was a new version of the 'Articles of Faith':

> I Beleeve in CROMWELL, the Father of all Schisme,
> Sedition, Heresy and Rebellion, and in his onely Son
> Ireton [Richard], our Saviour, begotten by the Spirit in
> a hole, borne of a winching Mare ... He [Cromwell]
> deserves to be drawn, hang'd and quartered, and to
> remain unburied: for he descended into Hull, the third
> day he rose up in Rebellion against his KING, and now
> sitteth at the right hand of the gods at Westminster. He
> beleeves there is no Holy Ghost, nor Catholique
> Church, nor forgiveness of sins, but the Communion
> of Sisters, the resurrection of Members, and Parliament
> everlasting. AMEN.

Another sheet was 'The Parliament's PATER
NOSTER':

> Our Fathers, which think your Houses of Parliament to
> be Heaven; you would be honoured as GODS, because
> CHARLES his Kingdom is come unto you; your wills
> must be done on earth, as unto the God of Heaven;
> you will have gotten the day, and dispose of our daily
> bread; you will not forgive any, neither must you look
> to be forgiven; you lead us into rebellion and all other
> mischiefs, but cannot deliver us from evil. Yours is the
> Kingdom, the power and glory, Parliament everlasting.
> AMEN.

A third sheet was a parody of the Ten Commandments:
Thou shalt have no other Gods but the LORDS and COMMONS assembled at Westminster. Thou shalt not make any Addresses to the King, nor yeeld obedience to any of his commands; neither shalt thou weare any Image either of him or his Posterity; thou shalt not bow down unto him, nor Worship him, for Wee are jealous Gods ... Thou shalt get all thou canst; part from nothing; doe no right, take no rong, neither pay any Debts ... Thou shalt be a Witness for us, against whomsoever wee judge to be Wicked, so that Wee may cut them off ... Thou shalt enjoy thy Neighbour's House, his Wife, his Servant, his Maid, his Oxe, or his Asse, or any thing that belongs unto him; Provided he first be Voted (by Us) to be a wicked or ungodly Person ...

However, there were not many ·satires as hard-hitting as these. Most of the great number of humorous publications of the period were collections of ballads and anecdotes – often downright bawdy – about peasants and parsons, fools and rogues, errant wives and drunken husbands, country lads and wenches, lords and judges; political satire or social criticism was apparently regarded as having no entertainment value. Yet a few of these stories would nowadays rank as black humour, such as the one about a witch at the stake who sees her son among the crowd and asks him for a drink of water. 'No, mother,' he says, 'it will do you no good, for the drier you are the better you'll burn!'
After the Restoration, anti-clerical jokes were on the wane, but there was one that might be interpreted that way: A lady hires a country girl as her new maid and asks her about her religion. 'Alas, madam,' says the girl, 'I never troubled my head about that. Religion, I thought, was only for gentlefolks.'
England's two outstanding satirists of the early eighteenth century, Daniel Defoe and Jonathan Swift,

have by a strange twist of literary history become famous
as the authors of children's books, *Robinson Crusoe* and
Gulliver's Travels. Yet writing for young readers was far
from the authors' minds; both saw their main task as
attacking the reaction, corruption and hypocrisy of their
contemporaries, and their bitter humour exerted great
influence on public opinion. Defoe, in particular, stirred
up a series of heated controversies. His first satire, *The
True-Born Englishman* (1701), assailed the xenophobia
which made certain sectors of the population object to
King William III's Dutch nationality, claiming the English
people's 'purity of blood'. In fact, Defoe reminded them,
they were a most 'composite' nation, a mixture of Celts,
Saxons, Danes, Normans and a few more foreign tribes.

A year later he published his pamphlet *The Shortest Way
with the Dissenters*, which made him notorious. Allegedly
written by a 'high-flying' churchman, it proposed a new
Bartholomew's Day massacre as the most practical way of
getting rid of the troublesome non-conformists. Defoe
had the great satisfaction of seeing the Church party
swallow the bait completely; they took the hoax seriously
as a possible solution of the problem, until some of the
more critical clerics understood that the anonymous
author had written a stinging satire on the Church's
intolerance. Defoe found himself in the pillory for
seditious libel – not an altogether unpleasant experience,
for the people of London demonstrated that they were
on his side, and newsvendors sold them the offending
pamphlet right under the guards' noses.

Swift, too, liked to clothe his satire in bogus proposals,
such as the suggestion that the hungry poor should eat
their children. His famous *Tale of a Tub* (1704) was a
denunciation of the 'corruption in religion and learning',
while *Gulliver's Travels* (1726), that beloved 'children's
book', was in fact an attack on the institutions and
attitudes of his time, unworthy of intelligent human
beings, on a wide front. His description of the land of the
Houyhnhnms, a race of horses endowed with the finer
characteristics of man, is an even more caustic social

criticism than Gulliver's accounts of his journeys to the Lilliputians and the giants of Brobdingnag. It was only in Victorian times that this masterpiece of satirical humour was watered down to a harmless fairy-tale for the young; Swift's serious message – that man's actions are a disgrace to the human race – has thus been lost.

While Britain had her own problems of succession, new wars of succession were fought on the Continent, making the biggest powers even bigger. A *bon mot* ascribed to the leading French General, Prince Eugène of Savoy – who fought in most of these wars, sometimes for his country but often against it – was this: 'We Generals are in the same situation as the great monarchies. The more weight we put on, the weaker we become.'

Only Prussia, a newcomer in European power politics, seemed to grow stronger with every conquest, especially under her acquisitive King Frederick 'the Great'. He also introduced a new concept – new at least in Germany – by inspiring his soldiers with the idea of national honour. During the Seven Years' War which Frederick, with England as his ally, fought against half a dozen European countries, this story circulated in the Habsburg Empire:

An Austrian officer captures a Prussian one. Haughtily, the prisoner sneers, 'We Prussians fight for our honour, but you Austrians fight only for money!'

'Why not?' retorts the Austrian. 'After all, each of us fights for what he needs most.'

This anecdote was told again half a century later, but then the Prussian had been changed into a French officer fighting for honour under Napoleon.

Another story from the Seven Years' War which was revived, with a few changes, in Napoleonic times was the one about the peasant who comes to a Prussian Colonel and complains that a gang of soldiers has attacked and robbed him:

'What did they take from you?' asks the Colonel.

'My purse, my coat and my shoes,' groans the peasant.

'Oh, then it must have been those darned Austrians,' says the Colonel. 'If it had been my Prussians, they would have taken your shirt as well.'

The version told in 1815 ran like this:

Three soldiers of the Allied armies, a Prussian, an Austrian and a Russian, happen to share the same quarters. When they are marching the next day, the Prussian says, 'Did you see the beautiful little clock on the mantelpiece? I wanted to put it in my knapsack, but that was already full.'

'Wait a minute, mates, I'll go back and get it,' says the Austrian.

'No use,' says the Russian. 'I've got it already.'

One hundred and fifty years later, a similar story was told in Poland about Kosygin and Brezhnev (see the last chapter): proof enough that Europe's image of the Russians did not change in all that time.

In its initial stages, the French Revolution had a strong anti-clerical character, and all kinds of jokes about the revenge the poor people took on the wealthy Church were told in France. One of the most popular stories concerned a group of peasants from a village in Picardy who appear before the Convention in Paris, bringing with them a cartload of gold and silver statuettes from their local church. 'We asked these saints,' explains a peasant, 'whether they would like to be melted down for the Revolution – they didn't say no!'

On the other side of the political fence, stories about the pride and courage of the doomed noblemen made the rounds, some sentimental, some sarcastic like this one: An aristocrat, condemned to death, stumbles on the steps leading up to the guillotine. 'A bad omen,' he remarks. 'An ancient Roman would have turned back.'

Europe's nobility was, of course, appalled and frightened by the French Revolution, not only by its bloody excesses but also by the speed with which the *ancien régime* was overthrown. Certainly, the revolutionary ideals of liberty, equality and fraternity appealed strongly to the intelligentsias of other countries, but in much of

Europe the upper classes insisted on hanging on to the old French traditions, manners and even language. This snobbery was especially widespread in Germany, whose western neighbour had always been looked upon as the homeland of refinement and gracious living.

Among the ordinary German people the 'francomania' of their betters was the cue for many jokes. In one, the young lady of the manor has been thrown from her horse; she picks herself up quickly, tidies her dress, and calls out to the groom, 'Did you observe my *agilité*, Johann?'

'I saw it all right,' he replies, 'but I didn't know that that's what they call the thing now!'

Napoleon, the upstart from Corsica, was ridiculed in many anecdotes – sometimes as a Frenchman, sometimes as an Italian. On the Pasquino statue in Rome there appeared this gibe in the then customary form of question and answer: '*E vero che tutti Francesi sono ladri?*' (Is it true that all Frenchmen are thieves?) '*Tutti, no, ma buona parte.*' (Not all of them, but a great many – a pun on Napoleon's surname.) In fashionable circles a similar story, this time calling him an Italian, ridiculed his notorious lack of social graces. An Italian lady dances with him at a court ball, and he points to some of her compatriots, remarking, '*Tutti gli Italiani danzano si male!*' (All Italians dance so badly), whereupon the lady answers with the same words: '*Tutti, no, ma buona parte.*'

To Madame de Staël, the daughter of a former French Minister of Finance and herself a prominent writer, Napoleon was said to have complained, 'I can't stand women meddling in politics.' She replied, 'Sire, in a country where women have been sent to the guillotine you can't blame them for asking why this happens to them.'

As the Napoleonic wars dragged on, the people in French-occupied Europe grew annoyed about the lack of initiative and unified planning among the Allies – mainly Prussia, Austria and Russia – in their campaigns against the Emperor. 'The Allies are always late by one idea, one army, and one month,' was a popular verdict. In France, however, people ridiculed the dozens of little kingdoms and duchies of Germany, most of which had declared war on Napoleon. A nice satirical story was that about the German prince who summoned the French envoy, handed him the declaration of war, and told him: 'I give you twenty-four hours to get out of my country.' The Frenchman bowed courteously and replied, 'Your Highness is too gracious. A quarter of an hour would be quite sufficient.' One of these pocket-size countries had as its heraldic beast a rearing horse. 'Why rearing?' asked the wags. 'Because if it stood on its four legs, the front ones would be already outside the country,' was the answer.

After Napoleon's first defeat, the Bourbons were put back on the throne of France; unwisely, the Allies sent Napoleon into exile on the island of Elba, only ten kilometres off the Italian mainland. He promptly escaped, returned to France, and started on a triumphal march to Paris. Masses of Frenchmen, especially the lower classes, cheered their beloved emperor on his way, and many veterans of his campaigns joined his troops. In Paris, the people shouting 'Vive l'Empereur' did not wave their handkerchiefs as the crowds had done when Louis XVIII had entered the capital some months before. The story goes that Napoleon asked Fouché, his Minister of Police, about the reason. 'Sire,' answered Fouché, 'the people who are now shouting "Vive l'Empereur" have no handkerchiefs.'

That was early in 1815. In June came Waterloo, which cost the French 40,000 men. Napoleon was captured and, to make sure there would be no new escape, sent to remote St Helena. The French, now in a more sober and sarcastic mood after two decades of imperialistic frenzy, composed a mock epitaph for him:

> *Passant! Ne plains pas mon sort.*
> *Si je vivais, tu serais mort.*
> ('Passer-by, do not grieve for me.
> If I were still alive, you'd be dead.')

When he did die a few years later, Talleyrand, the cynic who had served under three regimes, was said to have quipped, 'Just a news item, not an event.' But when Talleyrand himself died in 1838, European politicians asked, 'Now what did he intend by that, the old fox?'

2

From the Charivari to the Cabaret

Hogarth and Gillray, Cruikshank and Rowlandson developed social and political satire into a new form of pictorial art, the cartoon, in eighteenth and nineteenth-century England. Now verbal humour had a powerful ally for its attacks on misrule and unfairness, stupidity and injustice in public affairs. But the English brand of satire was never a weapon of revolution as in other countries; it was mainly used against persons in high places, including the monarch, who did not come up to the nation's expectations. King George III, who lost the American colonies, and his son, the Prince Regent and later George IV, were favourite targets of the caricaturists, the lampoonists and the pamphleteers.

There was nothing courageous in attacking the king and his favourites of both sexes in Georgian times; no press law or censorship such as in royal France and Prussia shielded the high and mighty. At least until the end of the first two decades of the nineteenth century, Britons could exercise their right to express their opinions in speech, writing or art without fear or hindrance. Ministers were freely savaged but could do little about it. Men in the public limelight 'threatened, prosecuted, wooed, and employed' satirists, as a literary historian put it; and Horace Walpole wrote, 'If satirical prints could dispatch them [Charles James Fox and Lord North], they would be dead in their cradle; there are enough to hang a room.' Prosecutions were started only for blasphemy, and there were very few legal actions for defamation – the satirists' victims knew quite well that court cases would make them even more ridiculous than the satire itself.

But things changed radically after the Peterloo Massacre of 1819. Sixty thousand people demonstrated peacefully in St Peter's Fields, Manchester, against the government's general neglect of the working classes' vital interests and in particular against the infamous Corn Laws. The banners they were carrying proclaimed their demands with slogans such as 'Vote by Ballot', 'Labour is the Source of Wealth', 'No Corn Laws', 'Equal Representation or Death', 'Success to the Female Reformers'.

Without any provocation, the crowd was attacked by the yeoman cavalry, police and hussars with rifles and sabres; eleven demonstrators were killed and 500 wounded. The nation was appalled. From then on, the fear of revolution prompted the government to adopt measures which we would nowadays ascribe to a police state: political meetings, especially those of the radicals, were restricted or prohibited; the press was closely watched; banishment was introduced for repeated publication of seditious or blasphemous matter; and vendors of oppositional journals were often jailed and occasionally flogged.

An 'underground' press now emerged, however, and caustic lampoons, under fictitious pen-names, were secretly printed. Even death served as a cue, as in this savage attack on the Prince Regent, shortly after George III's demise in 1820:

> Blinded with grief, or more probably brandy
> Were the eyes of this runagate elderly dandy.

What a welcome for a new king!

And what a difference between the British public's low opinion of their kings in the Georgian era and the sudden wave of sympathy for the young queen who ascended the throne in 1837. At first, the radical critics tried to make the most of Victoria's sex. 'We are now under petticoat government,' wrote a new London weekly, the *Penny Satirist*. 'Long live the British hen! And may we all be piously resigned to our fate as a henpecked nation!' Yet only a few weeks later, the same journal had to admit that Victoria had 'converted a great many radicals already', and it ended its comment on this tolerant note: 'We know one sour old scoundrel who has not blessed either king or queen for twenty years, who actually exclaimed when he saw her, "God bless the sweet creature, may she live long and happy!" We consider this one of the signs of the times.'

In France, young Honoré Daumier began his career as a cartoonist with the country's first satirical journal, *Charivari*, launched in 1832. The name spoke for itself: it meant a noisy peasant rumpus at weddings of unpopular villagers; though the custom was banned by the Church, it still continued. So the Parisians knew what they could expect from their new journal; they were not disappointed.

Daumier's favourite target was Louis Philippe of Orléans, the 'Citizen King' who had sided with the republicans in his youth and was invited to ascend the throne after the revolution of 1830; but he turned out to be an illiberal bungler. Daumier liked to caricature him as a pear because of the shape of his head. That pear became enormously popular; people talked about 'the pear' when they meant the King, and street urchins drew its outlines on walls and fences. Daumier was imprisoned for *lèse-majesté*, and *Charivari* got a heavy fine; it was paid for by the illegal sale of leaflets, drawn by Daumier, which showed Louis Philippe's face changing to a pear in four phases. The 1848 revolution drove the King into exile in England, where he died two years later.

Britain's great national humorous weekly was sub-titled 'The London Charivari' because the idea was to model it on the Paris journal, though its main title was thoroughly English – *Punch*. However, its basic aim was that of being comic without being rude. It was started in 1841 by a group of men associated with writing and the graphic arts. Mark Lemon, who had tried his hand at all kinds of business and had lately run an artists' and journalists' pub near the Drury Lane theatre in London, became the first editor of *Punch*, and its longest-serving one – for almost thirty years. He never aspired to make it a journal for militant political satire. 'All our ideas connected with *Punch* are happy ones,' said Lemon, and his advice to social reformers was: 'Destroy the principle of evil by increasing the means of cultivating the good, and the gallows will then become as much a wonder as it is now a jest.'

Still, in its early years the journal was radical and liberal, denouncing social evils, humbug and hypocrisy in public life, though it did so with good-natured humour. But there was, around 1850, a time when it indulged in anti-Semitic and anti-Catholic jokes. There were strong protests, and Richard Doyle, the journal's leading cartoonist and a devout Catholic, resigned. This taught Mark Lemon a lesson, and as he wanted not only the best English writers and artists as contributors but also the widest possible readership, his editorial policy from then on was that there should be no tactless idiosyncrasies. He got Tennyson, Thackeray and W. S. Gilbert to write for *Punch*, and John Leech, George du Maurier and John Tenniel were among the artists. Charles Dickens offered him only a single contribution, which was rejected.

Occasionally, *Punch* chimed in with general criticism of the government, e.g. of its scandalous mismanagement of the Crimean War, when the troops at the front were grossly neglected:

'Well, Jack,' says one soldier to his comrade in a Leech cartoon of 1856, 'here's good news from home. We're going to have a medal.'

'That's very kind,' comments the other soldier. 'Maybe one of these days we'll have a coat to stick it on.'

For over thirty years after the Continent's liberation from Napoleon, people had been waiting in vain for the fulfilment of their rulers' promises that the old autocratic regimes would be replaced by constitutional democracies. In March 1848, public anger boiled over in Central Europe: in Vienna, the domineering, reactionary State Chancellor Metternich was forced to resign, and he fled to England; in Munich, the masses made their art-loving King Ludwig I abdicate – he had incurred their indignation by his liaison with the extravagant dancer Lola Montez; in Berlin, the opening shots of the rebellion were fired by the citizens at the royal palace. 'We were all lying on our stomachs,' King Frederick William IV confessed later. He had a plaintive appeal, 'To my dear Berliners', posted all over the town; it betrayed his utter ignorance of his subjects' frame of mind, alleging that they were being 'led astray by a gang of villains, most of them foreign agents.' What the people really wanted was a German Republic. When their mood did not change and the barricades went up in Berlin, the King called out his artillery against the rebels. A grenade which had failed to explode got stuck in the casing of a pump, and some wit chalked on it, 'To my dear Berliners!'

That was the time when the popular humour of the Berliners, proverbial to this day, flourished; it had a splendid mouthpiece, the satirical writer Adolf Glassbrenner. His comical sketches were frequently enacted by amateur players in the inns and beer gardens, for instance a fair-crier's speech: 'And now, ladies and gentlemen and contemporaries, I'm going to show you the German Republic! Please come nearer and have a good look. What, you can't see anything? That's just it, ladies and gentlemen. If you can't see it, that's our German Republic!'

The year 1848 gave birth to Germany's first satirical-political journal called *Kladderadatsch* (meaning something like 'crash' or 'fiasco'); at first devoted to the cause of the revolution, it later deteriorated into a tame comic paper and died peacefully, eighty-five years old, when

Hitler came to power.

There were noisy days and nights also in the provinces. In Stuttgart, people told each other this story: The door bell rings at the house of Württemberg's Minister of State, Duvernoy, in the middle of the night. The servants are already in bed, and the minister opens the door himself. He faces a wildly excited citizen who cries, 'Herr Minister, you must call out the guards at once – there's such an uncanny silence in the town tonight!'

The 1848 revolutionaries came mostly from the liberal bourgeoisie, with students manning the barricades. In Paris, where unrest erupted in the same year, Louis Philippe was forced to abdicate. A republic was declared, and Louis Napoleon, a nephew of the late Emperor, was elected President. He was a cunning and ambitious schemer. In 1851, the 'Eagle', as he liked to be called, plotted a *coup d'état* to seize supreme power. On the night before, he was pacing his room, nervously puffing at his cigar. 'Do not worry, sir,' said his aide-de-camp, trying to calm him. 'One way or the other, you'll have a guard outside your door tomorrow night.'

Louis Napoleon's coup succeeded, and a year later France was a monarchy again, with him as Emperor Napoleon III. One of his first acts was the confiscation of the estates belonging to the rival house of Orléans, and a splendid pun among the Franch was: '*C'est le premier vol de l'aigle*' – *vol* meaning 'flight' but also 'theft'. Twenty years later, the 'Eagle' was defeated, deposed and imprisoned by the victorious Germans.

England's Industrial Revolution produced some caustic jokes. One from the middle of the last century had a manufacturer showing a friend round his new factory:

'It looks to me like the Passion in reverse,' said the visitor.

'What do you mean?' asked the manufacturer.

'Well, in the Passion one man suffered for everybody, and here everybody suffers for one man.'

A wealthy businessman, went another story, had his portrait painted. The artist depicted him with his hands

ostentatiously thrust in his pockets. The great man
showed the painting to his relatives:

'Not a very good likeness,' said one of them.

'Why not?'

'Because usually you have your hands in other people's
pockets.'

Ireland's poverty was the subject of this anecdote:

An Irish labourer praises his homeland in a London
pub, 'You can get a whole turkey for sixpence,' he says.

'But mate, why didn't you stay in that wonderful
country where you can buy a turkey for sixpence?' asks a
Londoner.

'And where do I get that sixpence?' asks the Irishman.

There were a few stories about the fight against slavery
in America before the Civil War. Very popular was this
one concerning Wendell Phillips, the famous abolitionist
reformer and orator from Boston. During a lecture tour
in Ohio he found himself in a railway compartment amid
some clergymen returning from a convention. One
minister, a southerner, recognized Phillips and tried to
provoke him:

'So you want to free the niggers?'

'Yes, sir,' replied Phillips.

'Well, why do you preach your doctrines up here? Why
don't you go down to Kentucky?'

'Tell me, sir, you are a preacher?' asked Phillips.

'I am.'

'And you try to save souls from hell?'

'Yes, that's my business,' said the minister.

'So why don't you go there?'

There is a good deal of black humour in Edgar Allan
Poe's work, and in some quips from Abraham Lincoln
which were widely quoted in the States. But the blackest
'joke' was the alleged question of a reporter after that
tragic theatre night of 14 April 1865: 'Apart from that,
Mrs Lincoln – how did you like the play?'

President Woodrow Wilson, who was out of favour
with certain sectors of the Senate and the American
public after the First World War, fell ill in 1919. A

Senator congratulated him on his recovery, telling him, 'We've all been praying for you.' 'Which way?' asked the President.

After their victory over France in 1871, the German states united at last under Prussia's leadership, with the Prussian King as the German Emperor. The new Central European power began to dominate Continental politics, and its architect, Bismarck, was the hero of the day and of many anecdotes, most of them invented and put into circulation by his nationalist admirers. The dream of 1848, of a liberal and democratic Republic of Germany, had evaporated in the heat of a chauvinistic and militaristic ecstasy.

Almost from the moment of his succession to the imperial throne in 1888, Wilhelm II, the 'young Kaiser', was the subject of innumerable jokes. His arrogance and ignorance, his ham-fisted and sword-rattling clumsiness in politics prompted Bismarck to his well-known remark: 'He behaves like a dachshund who has pulled down the tablecloth with everything on it, wags his tail and wants to be praised.' When the Kaiser sacked Bismarck in 1890, *Punch* published its famous and prophetic cartoon with the caption, 'Dropping the pilot'.

The German courts of law were kept busy with cases of *lèse-majesté*; many German newspapers and journals had their *Sitzredakteur*, a nominal editor who took the blame when a charge was brought against the paper and went to jail if that was unavoidable. The journal which got into trouble more frequently than any other was the satirical weekly *Simplicissimus*, founded in Munich in 1896. It was often banned by the censor because of its anti-Kaiser jokes and cartoons.

In order to avoid such encounters with the authorities, the satirists invented a pseudonymous character called Serenissimus as the archetype of a blockheaded monarch, a stand-in not only for Wilhelm but for any of the twenty-odd German princes as well as for the Austro-

Hungarian Emperor Franz Joseph. Serenissimus stories were told throughout Central Europe.

Freud, in his essay on jokes, relates this Serenissimus anecdote: The prince condescends to visit a hospital, where the head surgeon lets him attend the amputation of a man's leg. Every stage of the operation is applauded by the visitor with princely expressions of satisfaction: 'Bravo, bravo, my dear Professor!' When the job is completed, the surgeon bows to the distinguished observer and asks him, 'Is it your Serene Highness's command that I should now remove the other leg as well?'

Another Serenissimus story concerns his cross-country trip in the state coach. They come to the bottom of a steep hill, where the coachman harnesses two more horses to the prince's carriage. At the top of the hill the two extra horses are left behind, and Serenissimus muses, 'I suppose that in the course of time a great number of horses will have accumulated on that hill top!'

One Serenissimus joke was clearly aimed at the old Emperor Franz Joseph. He goes hunting; of course he misses with every shot, but his entourage are prepared for this. After he has fired on an eagle, they produce such a bird, congratulating His Majesty. But he is suspicious.

'That's not an eagle,' he declares. 'A real eagle has two heads!' (For the only bird of that species he knows is the double eagle of his imperial coat-of-arms, symbolizing Austria and Hungary.)

The Serenissimus joke which Freud analyses – he deals with it several times in his work – is this: the prince makes a tour through his provinces and notices a man who bears a striking resemblance to his own exalted person.

'Was your mother at some time in service at the palace?' he asks him.

'No, your Highness,' replies the man, 'but my father was.'

Freud apparently was not aware that this Serenissimus anecdote is in fact one of the evergreens which have been used as satirical come-backs at various times in history.

Macrobius, the philosopher who lived around AD 400, records it as an anti-Augustus joke: a young gentleman comes to Rome, and the Emperor, surprised at the man's likeness to himself, asks that same question and gets the same answer – a repartee which Freud calls 'an unexpected counter-attack' by which the prince's insult could be 'safely avenged'.

The Hohenzollern's most characteristic product was the Prussian soldier with his blind obedience, the symbol of German militarism. An often-told story is set on the Potsdam drill-ground where an NCO is training a recruit to do the perfect goose-step, yelling his commands at the man. Suddenly the NCO is called away and forgets to shout '*Halt!*' at the soldier. When he returns after a while, the man has disappeared. Thirty-three years later, an old soldier with a long, grey beard and in a ragged uniform marches into the drill-ground, still goose-stepping as well as he can. He has been marching around the globe because he was not commanded to stop.

In the heyday of the German Empire, the middle and upper classes grew rich while the workers and peasants remained poor. Scandals among the aristocracy were hushed up, but the little offenders were severely punished. 'They call it larceny only if it's under 100 marks,' was a popular quip. Heinrich Zille, Berlin's greatest cartoonist of the early 1900s, devoted himself to depicting the miserable lives of the city's poor with bitter humour. One of his masterpieces showed an emaciated woman leading her blind husband along the street, followed by some children in rags. They are just passing an undertaker's shop. 'What a pity you can't see that sweet little coffin,' she says to him. 'Just the right size for our dear Lotti – if we could afford it.' Another Zille caption became a proverbial saying in Berlin: the drawing showed a paralysed small girl in one of Berlin's typical slum backyards; her brother calls to their mother in the basement flat: 'Mum, put our flower pot on the window sill – our Lisa loves sitting in the green.'

The Bavarians, known for their rustic sense of

humour, rarely made jokes about their kings. They loved
especially Ludwig II, who patronized Richard Wagner
and took his own life in madness. The prince who should
have succeeded him was so insane that he had to be
locked up, and in his place Bavaria got an old Prince
Regent, kindly and only slightly gaga. That was the
period when Munich got its favourite song, by some
anonymous poet or poets, lampooning the entire
Bavarian establishment from the Prince Regent and the
whole royal family down to the monks, as they all pass by
in the annual Corpus Christi procession. It is a song with
innumerable stanzas because it makes fun of all the
marchers' and riders' foibles, fads, weaknesses and
scandals, and it is still being sung in the Bavarian capital
though the people and institutions it satirizes have gone
long ago.

One of the most efficient modern media for making
heard the voices of political and social critics was born in
Paris in the early 1880s: the cabaret. It was, however, a
somewhat tame child in its infant years. The first
establishment of this kind was the *Chat Noir*, the Black Cat,
in Montmartre, more an artists' café than a forum for
satire; there was no fixed programme since the accent
was on improvisation. The Parisians flocked to the *Chat
Noir* to be shocked by macabre ballads and insulted by
ragged-trousered bohemians.

Gradually, satire about topical events and personalities
entered the programme. Once, the notorious War
Minister General Boulanger, the would-be dictator and
propagandist of a *revanche* war against Germany, sat in
the audience while a chanson attacked him from the
stage, with the punch-line: 'France can well manage
without any more Generals!'

A *Chat Noir* regular, the working-class artiste Aristide
Bruant, opened his own cabaret, one of many that were
now springing up all over Montmartre and the Quartier
Latin. But Bruant became and remained the most

famous cabaretist. He was an anarchist and delighted in provoking his mainly bourgeois audience with his chansons about the victims of social injustice, about the jobless, the whores, the *clochards* in the gutter. Bruant's lyrics were quoted throughout Paris, and his style established the political cabaret tradition in France and soon also in Central Europe. His most famous disciple was Yvette Guilbert, one of the first women on the miniature stage which had been dominated by men in its early years.

Around the turn of the century, Munich was Germany's artistic and cultural centre, and it was here that the country's cabaret evolved, in fact as a protest movement against an infamous new law. This so-called *Lex Heinze* gave the German police the power to proscribe works of art, from paintings to plays, if they were considered dangerous to public morals. During the carnival of 1901, a group of secessionist artists, students, actors and writers, among them the dramatist Frank Wedekind, together with members of the *Simplicissimus* editorial staff paraded through the streets in fancy dress, carrying rebellious posters denouncing the new law and police censorship.

Eleven of the demonstrators stayed together to launch a cabaret, which they called *Die 11 Scharfrichter*, the Eleven Executioners. They hired a small theatre, decorated it with grotesque masks and torture instruments, and opened it as a members-only club to avoid trouble with the police because of their daring programmes.

The tone of the enterprise was set from the start, with travesties of moralist literature, parodies of chauvinistic authors and satires on the Kaiser's insane ambitions. Here, the first star of the German cabaret was born: Marya Delvard, tall and thin, red-haired and wide-mouthed, usually dressed in black. One of her greatest successes was Frank Wedekind's melancholy song about the girl who, at fifteen, had been introduced to 'love's sweet, intoxicating taste' and remained an addict ever since, with the final lines:

'When I no longer rouse desire,
Well, then I might as well be dead.'

These verses would never have passed the censor. Wedekind had already spent six months in jail a year before, sentenced for *lèse-majesté* because he had ridiculed the Kaiser's journey to Palestine in a ballad published in the *Simplicissimus*.

The Executioners did not stay together for long, but their influence on Central Europe's artists and poets, who were fighting a continuous battle with the censor, was enormous. Marya Delvard and another member of the Munich cast went to Vienna where they opened the city's first cabaret, the *Nachtlicht* or night-light, later renamed the *Fledermaus* after Johann Strauss' operetta. It was the Austrian capital's *belle époque*, with imperial splendour and extravagance on the one hand and a flourishing literary and artistic life on the other. Although the emphasis of the Viennese cabaret was on elegant and whimsical humour, the almost religious adoration of the Austro-Hungarian army did not escape the cabaretists' satire. One snatch of dialogue from a cabaret programme became a popular Viennese joke:

'... And there's our beautiful army. Wouldn't it be a pity if it were sent out to fight?'

'Yes, it would, but what else should we do with it in a war?'

'Simply withdraw it, right back into the heart of our country where it wouldn't come to any harm.'

'But then the enemy would march in, and we'd lose the war!'

'Sure, but we'd still have our beautiful army.'

It was sent to war after all, and its beauty crumbled in the trenches, in the Italian and Russian mud, on the mountains of the Balkans. Yet the rulers in Vienna would not believe that the Habsburg Empire was doomed; the bureaucrats and the politicians were as boneheaded as ever. Near the end of the First World War an anecdote which might well have been true was current among the

Viennese: Some time before the war the Austro-Hungarian government received a sharp note from St Petersburg, demanding that a stop be put to the activities of the Russian political emigrants in Vienna. The Minister of the Interior received the note and shook with laughter: 'Who do they think is going to start a revolution in Russia – perhaps that Herr Trotsky from the Café Central?'

A bulldog opening a champagne bottle with its teeth was the emblem of Munich's most famous early cabaret; it was a variation of the bulldog that had broken its chain, the emblem of the *Simplicissimus*, and the cabaret was given the same name as the journal. It was a modest place in Schwabing, the traditional quarter of Munich's artists, poets and bohemians; it consisted of two rooms crammed with tables and chairs and a narrow platform for the performers in the middle. The owner, Frau Kati Kobus, was a buxom former waitress from the countryside, usually dressed in a dirndl; she ruled the establishment with a certain strictness but was beloved by all the regulars. She allowed anyone who was not hopelessly drunk or raving mad to mount the podium and sing, recite or play what they liked.

Here, Bertolt Brecht tried out his first expressionist ballads, strumming a guitar; Erich Mühsam, the anarchist and poet who was to play a leading part in the Bavarian 'Soviet Republic' of 1919, recited his satirical verses; Joachim Ringelnatz, the ex-sailor, never quite sober, soon became the resident poet with his bawdy and irreverent rhymes.

Berlin had only a few respectable literary cabarets before the First World War, but in the Weimar era, when there was no more Wilhelminian censorship, political-satirical cabarets were shooting up like mushrooms after the rain. But before we survey the Berlin scene of that period, let us look at some developments before and during the war.

Britain never had the right political climate to encourage
cabarets as a framework for satire. Had there been any
cabarets in the early years of our century, the activities of
the suffragettes would have been a favourite topic in their
programmes. As it was, jokes about them abounded in
the newspapers and journals, nearly all making fun of the
movement. The suffragettes themselves, of course, did
not feel that their cause was a laughing matter. One story
which is still remembered tells of two suffragettes who
have been locked up; one breaks down and cries while
the other tries to console her: 'Cheer up, my dear. Put
your trust in God. She will help us!'

The First World War was no laughing matter either,
least of all for the French. Yet it says much for their
indomitable spirit that in 1915, with a large chunk of
their country in enemy hands, they launched a new
satirical journal which still enjoys a high reputation: *Le
Canard Enchaîné*, the fettered duck or, rather, canard.

There were some bitter anti-war rhymes in hungry,
blockaded Germany. One verse was chalked on many
walls, promising that peace would come when the Kaiser
wore a top hat instead of his spiked helmet and 'Guste',
his wife Augusta, had to queue up for potatoes. A couplet
circulating among the German soldiers at the front went
        'If all of us had equal grub and pay
        the war would hardly last another day.'

At home in Germany most public conveniences
showed, at some time or another, this widely popular
graffito:

        'Please wipe your arsehole with your hand,
        save paper for the fatherland!'

Zurich, neutral Switzerland's largest town, assumed a
certain importance during the First World War: it
became the international centre for a great number of
writers, artists and politicians who were appalled by the
butchery at the fronts and tried to shout some kind of
protest. Among them were the Frenchman Romain

Rolland, the Austrian Stefan Zweig, the Irishman James Joyce, Lenin and his wife Krupskaya, and some pacifist intellectuals and painters from Germany. Around them gathered several younger artists, poets and musicians, and it was almost a matter of course that they started a cabaret to express their views.

So, in 1916, the *Cabaret Voltaire* was launched – and with it one of the most eccentric literary and artistic movements: Dada. It was an attempt to give voice to the revulsion against the madness of war, the voice being that of a child who has not yet learnt to speak properly. Dada poetry and lyrics consisted of meaningless syllables, often accompanied by whistling, cow-bells, banging on tables, screams and sobs. Costumes were just as fantastic, strongly influenced by the cubist movement in art. At the *Voltaire* one could also hear some expressionistic 'prayers', performed by a young German poet and student of psychiatry, Richard Hülsenbeck, and accompanied by tom-tom beats; and the first bizarre collages by the artist Kurt Schwitters were exhibited.

It would be a gross overstatement to say that the goings-on at the *Voltaire* had much influence on public opinion, except that they put the staid Zurich citizens' backs up. They launched their own protest movement, and the cabaret had to close down after a short life-span. Dada spread to post-war Germany, however, where it was eventually overtaken by the surrealist movement. During its short but noisy heyday, Dada launched a curious journal entitled *Everyone his own Football*; its emblem was a photomontage by John Heartfield, showing a bowler-hatted man with a football as his body.

Berlin's Dadaists of 1919 included a number of artists and writers who later contributed much to Weimar culture. This was the era which began when the new German Republic's first legislative assembly met in that little Thuringian town which had once been the home of Goethe and Schiller. Weimar was chosen for the purpose because the capital, Berlin, was then in a state of prolonged unrest, with much streetfighting between the

Spartacists (who later called themselves Communists) and various bands of right-wing militants. Weimar was a peaceful backwater without industry and therefore without organized workers. It was here that the new republican Constitution of Germany was enacted, and thus the name of the town became that of the whole era.

Dada flourished in Berlin's violent climate for a year or two. Among the movement's protagonists were George Grosz, already known for his brilliant satirical drawings – he was the 'Propagandada'; Walter Mehring, later one of the leading cabaret lyricists, called the 'Pupidada' (whatever that was supposed to mean); two brothers, Wieland Herzfelde, later the publisher of new American and Soviet literature, and John Heartfield, the 'Monteur-Dada', who had anglicized his name by deed-poll during the war as a protest against the chauvinistic slogan, '*Gott strafe England*', of the Kaiser's propaganda machine. Heartfield was the creator of photomontage as a political medium. Schwitters and Hülsenbeck, who had both returned from Zurich, were also among the Dada activists in Berlin.

Dada, calling itself modestly the 'Headquarters of the World Revolution', was in evidence all over the town, with parades in masks, grotesque dances, futuristic fairs, sticker campaigns, cabaret evenings with outrageous recitals, and demonstrations outside the government buildings. One Dada exhibition was dominated by the life-size stuffed effigy of a German officer with a pig's head, suspended from the ceiling with a placard, 'Hanged by the Revolution', around the neck. No wonder most of the Dadaists landed in jail, at least for a few days. Absurd and scurrilous though the movement was, it made its point against political reaction with its shock tactics.

Prague's first literary cabaret was the *Montmartre* on the Moldau Embankment. Franz Kafka was among its contributors; so was his friend, the poet and novelist Max

Brod, and the reporter Egon Erwin Kisch, who was to become the initiator of modern in-depth journalism. Another was Jaroslav Hašek, a war veteran, writer and bohemian, who was then working on a book that was to sweep the world with its anti-militarist satire, establishing one of the great comic heroes of literature: *The Good Soldier Shveyk* (or Schweik, to use the German spelling of the Czech name).

'This fellow's wise enough to play the fool,' says Shakespeare's Viola in *Twelfth Night*: perhaps the best characterization of the Good Soldier who, posing as a simpleton, fights the military bureaucracy of the Habsburg Empire by sly sabotage. He has been called a glorified coward, a cunning anarchist, or a Czech patriot helping his country's struggle for independence after three centuries of Austrian occupation – all these descriptions apply, but the work's enormous international success is no less due to its being one of the funniest books ever written.

Born in Prague in 1883, the son of a professor of mathematics, Hašek got his first job as a bank clerk but soon began to write short stories, publishing sixteen volumes of them before the 1914 war. He was well known in Prague as an eccentric; once he founded a mock-political 'Party of Moderate Progress within the Bounds of the Law'. He was conscripted into the Austrian army, sent to the Eastern front, and defected to the Russians; they used him as the editor of anti-Austrian journals, and eventually he joined the Red Army. When he returned home in 1921, Czechoslovakia was a free republic.

He began to write his *Shveyk*, which he planned in six volumes; it was published in short instalments and sold not only in the bookshops and at the newspaper kiosks, but also in the coffee-houses, inns, and beerhalls by itinerant vendors – including, it was said, the author himself. After completing about half of his gargantuan work, he died in 1923, and a Czech friend wrote the other half which, however, did not reach the comic and literary quality of the first. Right from the start, *Shveyk* was immensely popular among the Czechs, though the authorities frowned upon the book as it did not seem to cast a very sympathetic light on the Czech national character.

It was only in 1926, when the first translation (into German) appeared, that the outside world took notice of *Shveyk*; the great breakthrough came two years later when Erwin Piscator, the German left-wing producer, staged a brilliant theatrical adaptation of the work in Berlin's West End, with designs by George Grosz and John Heartfield. Now everybody read the book and it was translated into two dozen other languages. It was almost a pity that the Habsburg Empire no longer existed – *Shveyk* would have hastened its demise.

But Hitler did exist, and when he came to power, free, democratic Czechoslovakia was in mortal danger: it was among his priorities for annexation. Shveyk's spirit marched again; its best representatives were two Prague students who had started their satirical revues at university before turning professional, with their own theatre, in the mid-1930s: Voskovec and Werich, 'V & W' as they were called for short. Their political jokes – against Hitler, racism, social injustice and chauvinism – helped greatly to lift up the hearts of the Czechs, right until that fateful day in March 1939 when the Nazi jackboots tramped along the Wenceslas Square.

There was one story which probably originated in Prague in those tense days of the Czechoslovak crisis; it made its way all over Europe: a Sudeten–German Nazi exhorts the audience at a political meeting to 'return to the fatherland', meaning Hitler's Germany.

'What keeps you in this ridiculous little Czechoslovak Republic?' he asks.

A voice from the back row answers: 'Just one thing. When the door bell rings at seven in the morning, I know it's only the postman.'

'The Kaiser went, the Generals remained' – the title of a critical political book – was a popular saying in the

Weimar Republic. Many Germans who were well aware of the fragility of the Republic's democracy became increasingly worried about the strength of the old militaristic guard and its machinations behind the scenes. The Versailles Treaty of 1919 had banned Germany from rearming, yet secretly it was being done. A widely-told story summed up the situation: a Berlin worker at a factory for prams pinches all kinds of components over a few months, hoping to assemble a nice pram for the baby his wife is expecting; but in the end he complains, 'I don't understand it. Every time I put these parts together I get a machine-gun!'

Berlin grew into a cultural island, hated (and, of course, envied) in the German provinces because of its achievements in the arts, its cosmopolitanism and what was called its 'libertinism'. Perhaps Berlin's most characteristic indigenous art form in that era was the literary political cabaret – without a leg-show or elaborate decor and costumes, and with just a piano instead of an orchestra. Usually, such a place was a small hall, often a former café or bar, and the stage was only a bare podium; the audience sat at tables, eating and drinking during the performance. There were, at any time during the decade before Hitler took over, about two dozen cabarets of this kind in Berlin.

They were nearly all mouthpieces of the resistance against the rising tide of Nazism. Lyrics, dialogues and jokes, satirical and hardhitting, often made their way from the cabaret to the general public; vice versa, popular quips, skits and humorous stories were picked up by the cabaretists and included in their programmes. Hitler and his allies, the Generals and *Junkers*, hypocritical politicians and reactionary public figures were attacked, the smug bourgeois was kicked in the backside to make him sit up and understand what was happening behind the façade of the Republic's shaky parliamentary system.

Many lyrics by Kurt Tucholsky – 'a fat little Berliner who tried to stem the catastrophe with his typewriter', as

Erich Kästner put it – and by Kästner himself were set to
music and performed in the cabarets. In one of his most
caustic poems Kästner said:

> If we had won the war – good heavens! –
> with iron fists and flags unfurled,
> all Germany'd be at sixes and sevens
> and look like a madhouse to the world ...
> Then Reason would be kept in fetters
> and forced, at court, to kiss the rod.
> New fights would be run like operettas
> if we had won the war – however,
> we didn't win it, and thank God.

Friedrich Hollaender, who wrote and composed his
own satirical revues, called the cabaret 'a battlefield
where the clean weapons of sharpened words and loaded
music can beat those of murderous steel'. Bertolt Brecht,
Walter Mehring, Erich Mühsam and Joachim Ringelnatz
were among the poets whose verses were always sung in
the cabarets. The lyricist Marcellus Schiffer, who had
written two opera libretti for Hindemith, and the
popular composer Mischa Spoliansky created their own
brand of cabaret-revue: here was the very essence of
Berlin's saucy, smart, mischievous yet essentially
warmhearted wit. These revues were always about topical
themes, though they may have lacked the political
aggression of the smaller cabarets. In 1928, a twenty-
four-year-old actress with beautiful legs and a sexy, husky
voice joined the Schiffer–Spoliansky team – Marlene
Dietrich. This was her first chance to display in the
limelight her 'inimitable mixture of elegance and vulgar
smartness', as the critics called it.

The most famous, the most often quoted and certainly
the most courageous of Berlin's cabaretists was Werner
Finck, a lanky, bespectacled young man with a shy smile.
He started his little theatre, the *Katakombe*, in 1929, and
within a few weeks it became a symbol of the
intellectuals' fight for the Republic, against Hitler and
reaction. Finck, as the compère of the show, had a unique

knack of establishing at once an intimate, knowing relationship with his audience; often he would cut short his pointed sentences, yet everyone knew what he was getting at. He wrote his material himself. In one typical scene he was a somewhat dense law student, being examined by his professor who wants him to talk about diminished responsibility:

Professor: Now you often find in the court reports cases of defendants being acquitted though their offences are proven. Why? Not because they are minors or have acted in self-defence, but because – well, what?
Student (with brightening face): Because they are Nazis!

Stormtroopers were often sent to the *Katakombe* to heckle Finck, but they were no match for him. Once they shouted at him, 'Jewboy!' He smiled disarmingly: 'You are mistaken, I only look so intelligent.'

His cabaret managed to survive for two years under Hitler's rule. He took amazing risks. Eventually the Gestapo arrested the whole cast; Finck landed in a concentration camp. He was released only after signing the customary undertaking not to complain about his treatment behind barbed wire. Friends asked him what the food was like, and he replied, carefully: 'Like in a respectable family who, through no fault of their own, have got into rather straitened circumstances.' This became a classic Finck quote in Berlin.

3

Jokes Against Hitler and Mussolini

The lack of a sense of humour is a favourite prejudice which nations hold against each other. Usually, all it means is 'their sense of humour is not our sense of humour'. However, the nation charged all over the western world with a particular lack of that human quality has been Germany, at least during the last century or so.

It is, of course, not really true, though the reasons for that prejudice are historically interesting. First of all, if any of the German peoples who united in the Hohenzollern Empire in 1871 may be characterized as singularly lacking humour in their cultural life, it is the Prussians, who were after all dominant in the Wilhelminian era. Had it been the Austrians, the Bavarians, or the Rhinelanders, the image of the Germans as humourless would probably never have arisen; nor would it have if the Berliners, a 'tribe' of their own had been dominant: all have their special brands of humour in literature, on the stage and in daily life, but this German humour depends to a large extent on dialect and so does not travel well abroad.

Secondly, the principal means by which a nation's standard of humour can be judged is literature, and here the Germans present a rather poor show (again with the exception of the rich but wellnigh untranslatable dialect works). The German literary heritage contains no Molière or Jerome K. Jerome, no *Gargantua and Pantagruel* or *Moll Flanders*, no Cervantes or Mark Twain. The German classic *Simplicius Simplicissimus* from the Thirty Years' War, though a magnificent documentary of the time, is merely incidentally humorous. The only major humorous novel appeared in our own century: Thomas Mann's *Felix Krull*. However, Germany had a light-weight comic poet and artist in the last century, Wilhelm Busch, and early in our own one brilliant nonsense-verse writer, Christian Morgenstern; a Californian professor, Max Knight, achieved the miraculous feat of translating his *Gallows Songs* into English. Heinrich Heine, of course, was the outstanding satirical poet, but not much of his work has been translated into other languages. From Heine to the 1920s there is a great void until we find the satirical poets Erich Kästner and Kurt Tucholsky (see Chapter Two).

Thirdly, the German theatre produced hardly any comedies that might have proved to the world that the country's playwrights could write humorous works. Admittedly, Schiller and Lessing, Kleist and Gerhart Hauptmann wrote one or two each, but they were not masterpieces of international appeal. Goethe's *Faust* contains some flashes of splendid wit, and his rebellious knight Goetz von Berlichingen answers an Imperial officer's call to surrender with the blunt invitation to kiss his arse – an expletive that had the same shock effect in Germany as Eliza's 'bloody' in twentieth-century England. Yet it was not until fifty or sixty years ago that Carl Sternheim and Carl Zuckmayer wrote true comedies of lasting value for the German stage.

One reason for the lack of comedy on the German stage was without doubt the influence of Schiller, which lasted throughout the nineteenth century. In 1784 he published an essay, *The Theatre Regarded as a Moral Institution*, inspired by all the high-flown motivations of the *Sturm und Drang* movement but a heavy damper for any dramatist aspiring to the entertainment of his audience by humour and satire: if there was any entertainment at all, it had to be 'united with the education of the intellect and the heart'. From now on, no German tragedy was to contain any comic relief, and potential writers of comedy were scared off by the great Schiller's demand that they should follow only the divine call of their souls, 'serving the supreme interest of humanity', instead of 'wasting their talents on subjects of minor importance'.

However, the German theatre sidestepped that generally accepted ruling by producing Shakespeare's plays, especially when the magnificent translations by Schlegel and Tieck became available early in the nineteenth century. The German audiences adopted Shakespeare, the 'poetic humorist' (as Priestley called him), to all intents and purposes as a German playwright, as they later accepted Wilde and Shaw. One might, therefore, argue that the German sense of humour had been blocked up and intimidated by an authoritarian climate which branded wit as an un-German activity – only foreigners were permitted to make people laugh. Wilhelminian pomposity and chauvinist bombast were the characteristics of many German plays of the era after 1871.

The Weimar Republic brought to German writers the freedom to create and enjoy humour, and this ought to have shown the world that Germany was not lacking in humour. Alas, that period was pitiably short, to be followed by the humourless, humour-fearing Nazi regime in 1933. But German wit did not wither; it just went underground. And thus Hitler Germany became history's most productive source of political jokes.

The German Labour movement, the Social Democrats, had so little political foresight that they supported the election of the aged war leader General Field-Marshal Hindenburg as Reichs President, hoping that the 'grand old man' might be a suitable figure-head for the ship of state in the turbulent waters of the international economic crisis. But Hindenburg, by his background a

representative of the Prussian landowning class, the
Junkers, was already in a stage of advanced senility, and his
entourage had no difficulty in making him sign any
document without explaining to him what it was. This
was rather dangerous for the Republic, for a state of
emergency was declared more than once during
Hindenburg's tenure of office – which meant that new
laws and regulations were enacted not by Parliament but
by presidential decree.

A favourite Hindenburg story was about a journalist,
waiting for hours in the President's ante-room to be
admitted for an interview, who got so hungry that he
unpacked his sandwiches. Meissner, Hindenburg's
Secretary of State, discovers the journalist munching
away, with the sandwich wrappers lying on the table.
'For heaven's sake,' cries Meissner, 'take that away! If the
old man finds any piece of paper lying around, he'll sign
it.'

The last year of the Weimar Republic, 1932, was also its
maddest. One election followed another; there were,
thanks to the proportional-representation system, thirty-
odd parties, each promising to put an end to the civil-
war-like turmoil and to bring work to the six million
unemployed. Reichs governments were formed and
dissolved in quick succession. Finally, on 30 January 1933,
Herr von Papen – the most efficient gravedigger of the
Weimar Republic – made Hindenburg sign one more
document: the appointment of Hitler as Chancellor. The
Nazi regime began.

On that evening, Hitler celebrated his victory with an
enormous torch parade of his stormtroopers and
jackbooted SS men through the centre of Berlin.
Hindenburg was persuaded to come to the window of his
palais in the Wilhelmstrasse to watch the march-past. He
looked down in silence, and some dim reminiscence of
the Great War seemed to dawn on him. 'Amazing,' he
remarked, 'what a lot of Russian prisoners!' That was the
last joke to be told about Hindenburg.

With the Nazis in power, the character of Germany's

political humour changed fundamentally. The 'whispered joke' was born as newspapers, magazines and other instruments of public opinion were either shut down or taken over by Goebbels' men – which happened very quickly also to the radio stations. Many contributors and editors were sent to the concentration camps.

The trade unions were dissolved and replaced by the so-called Labour Front after the model of Mussolini's corporations. But that did not dispose of the eight million Social–Democratic and five million Communist sympathizers, the majority of them workers, who had voted in the last free elections. Where had they all gone? At the labour exchanges, officials now had to give priority to the 'veterans' of the Nazi movement. A Berlin worker, applying for a job, was asked whether he qualified as an 'old fighter'. 'All I can say,' was his reply, 'is that I already carried the red flag before they put a swastika in it.'

In the early days of the Nazi regime there was a story about Dr Ley, the Labour Front leader, visiting a large Berlin factory and asking the manager what he knew about the political sympathies of his workers:

'Well,' replies the manager, 'half of them are Social Democrats, a third are Communists, ten per cent belong to the Christian trade unions ...'

'What,' cries Dr Ley, 'aren't there any National Socialists?'

'Sure,' answers the manager, 'of course they're all Nazis.'

Those were the days when many unemployed workers joined the SA and put on the despised brown uniform just for safety's sake, and often for the mere prospect of a hot meal a day. 'What have a stormtrooper and an English beefsteak in common?' asked a jocular question. The answer: 'Both are brown outside and red inside.'

Another Berlin joke characteristic of that period was about a tramp who needs a roof over his head, even if it is only that of a prison cell. So he goes up to a policeman, shouts '*Rot Front!*'and raises his clenched fist. The policeman pretends not to have heard or seen anything and continues on his beat. A column of stormtroopers comes marching along, and the tramp repeats his performance. One of the SA men breaks rank and tells him off:

'Are you nuts, mate? There, in the third row, we've got a Nazi!'

The frustrated tramp decides to spend the night in a Tube station. As he walks down, an SS officer comes up. '*Rot Front!*', the tramp shouts again.

'Idiot,' hisses the SS man, 'can't you see I'm in uniform?'

Such jokes from the first year of the Nazi regime served a distinct purpose: they propped up the political and intellectual confidence of many Germans that the whole Hitler nightmare could not possibly last very long, by demonstrating that the country still contained millions of Anti-fascists, many of them in brown and black uniforms. In fact, Hitler himself was worried about the leftist, Socialist tendencies that the new recruits brought to his movement; and no less a danger to him were those 'veterans' in the leadership who were now expecting him to carry out his promise of action against capitalism and the reactionary bourgeoisie. But Hitler's hands were tied: those were the very sources of his movement's finances.

Things came to a head when the commander of the stormtroopers, Hitler's old comrade Röhm, seemed to be planning to turn them into an independent, anti-capitalist force. Hitler forestalled Röhm by having him seized and killed, together with great numbers of stormtroopers suspected of rebellious tendencies, and hundreds of other men who had once stood in his way. That was the 'night of the long knives' of 30 June 1934.

The most significant comment on that event was this story:

Two SA men meet in a prison cell. 'Why did they arrest you?' one asks the other.

'Because two days ago I was shouting, "Down with Röhm!" ' replies the man. 'And you?'

'Because yesterday I was shouting, "Long live Röhm!" ' answers the other.

This dialogue was revised and retold in Prague in 1952 when Slansky, the powerful Secretary of the Communist Party, had suddenly been deposed, arrested and branded as a traitor – and two loyal Party members were locked up on consecutive days for shouting the wrong slogans.

A priority project of the Nazi regime was the building of concentration● camps; Oranienburg near Berlin and Dachau near Munich were the first of hundreds. Weiss Ferdl, an immensely popular Munich comedian, dared to joke about that new institution. 'I took a walk around the Dachau camp,' he told his audience. 'Most impressive and well protected, I must say. The walls are ten metres high, with barbed wire along the top, electrically charged, and machine-gun towers at every corner – still, I only have to say a word or two, and I'll be inside in a jiffy!'

That story was told all over Germany, and so was a little scene enacted by Weiss' equally famous rival, Karl Valentin. He walked briskly onto the stage, raised his arm in the Nazi salute and shouted 'Heil' – then scratched his head and confessed, 'Dammit, now I've forgotten the name!'

Some anti-Nazi jokes in circulation were ascribed to these two comedians though they may never have told them, such as this one, which was later used against other regimes:

Valentin was said to have told his audience, 'This morning I saw a beautiful new Mercedes limousine stopping right in front of me. The door opened, and – you'll be surprised – it *wasn't* an SS officer who stepped out.'

Valentin was severely reprimanded by the Nazi authorities. 'Don't worry,' he promised, 'I'll put things right.'

The next evening he apologised to his audience for

having misled them: 'The truth is, it *was* an SS officer after all!'

This double-edged story was also told after the war in the US Occupation Zone of Germany, with an American officer stepping out of the Mercedes; and it is still being told in the GDR, the Communist part of Germany, about some *apparatchik* from the ruling clique.

Telling jokes about the Nazi regime was an increasingly dangerous occupation. You could do it only after looking over your shoulder to see whether anyone was in earshot – it was called the 'German look'. Werner Finck (see the previous chapter) had a sketch that became famous. It was set at the dentist's, where he is asked to open his mouth:

'Why just me, of all people?' retorts Finck as the patient.

'Now, now,' the dentist tries to calm him, 'don't be afraid and open your mouth!'

'Either one or the other,' says Finck.

There was a persistent rumour that Göring was circulating jokes against himself, about his love of medals and uniforms and his exhibitionism. The purpose, it was said, was to create an image of himself as a jolly, good-natured fellow with a few human weaknesses, to correct his reputation as a Nazi bully. He was even supposed to have promised a glass of beer to his chauffeurs for every joke about him they heard, with the result that they got drunk every day. One of these jokes said that he had to refuse to accept any more medals because if he covered the few empty places on his uniform he would no longer be able to sit down; another story reported that he had had his latest uniform made with a cellophane back so that the German people could see some meat for a change.

In his role as the great art lover he was said to have saved some Jewish artists from the concentration camps; and when Himmler, the SS leader, remonstrated with him about it he declared, 'I'm the one to decide who's a Jew and who isn't!' He may really have said that; but the

saying usually attributed to him, 'When I hear the word
Kultur I reach for my revolver', was in fact coined by one
of the few talented writers the Nazis could list among
their supporters, the former expressionist playwright
Hanns Johst.

One story about Göring – and Goebbels, the
Propaganda Minister – is unlikely to have originated
from the Luftwaffe Marshal himself: the pair have died
and are sent to hell. Their punishment: Göring gets a
thousand new uniforms but no mirror, Goebbels a
thousand radios but no microphone.

The older generation of the middle classes took quite a
while to accept the Nazi clique as Germany's new
government; revealing of their initially unfriendly
attitude to Hitler and his cronies was this joke: Hitler (or,
according to another version, Goebbels) takes a walk
through the woods around Berlin and falls into a lake.
Three Hitler Youths who happen to be passing by drag
the drowning man out and revive him.

Hitler: 'You've saved my life; you may ask for
anything – your wishes shall be granted.'

The first boy says he wants to be an airman; Hitler
promises to send him to a top training course. The
second boy wants to be an officer; he will be joining the
cadet corps. Only the third boy hesitates to state his wish;
eventually, he whispers:

'*Mein Führer*, I should like to have a state funeral.'

Hitler: 'But my boy, you are much too young to think
of a funeral!'

The boy: 'That's what you think, *mein Führer*. As soon
as my father finds out whom I've helped to rescue, he'll
wring my neck!'

Such 'underground' stories became a fact of life in the
Third Reich, and their existence was taken for granted by
everybody; they were generally called *Flüsterwitze*,
whispered jokes. One described a scene in a tramcar: two
men are making strange gestures to each other, then they
suddenly burst out laughing. 'What on earth are they
doing?' one passenger asks another. 'They are deaf-and-

dumb,' is the answer. 'They are telling each other
political jokes!'

In 1935, the Nazi government introduced its infamous
'race laws', officially called 'Laws for the Protection of the
German Blood'. They stipulated that only people of the
'Aryan' race could be German citizens, thus outlawing all
Jews, gypsies and other people of 'alien' origin. Anyone
whose ancestry was doubtful had to furnish proof of his
or her 'pure' extraction. A great search for 'Aryan
grannies' began. One whispered joke re-told the fairy
story of Little Red Riding Hood: She meets the big bad
wolf in the forest. 'Where are you going?' asks the wolf.
'I'm looking for my grandmother,' replies the girl.
'Aren't we all?' sighs the wolf.
    Those Jews who had still remained in Germany were
now seriously considering emigration. 'Are you an
Aryan,' friends asked one another, 'or are you learning
English?' The crunch came in November 1938, after a
young Polish Jew had shot an official at the German
embassy in Paris, and the Nazi leadership immediately
organized a 'spontaneous' attack on Jewish homes, shops
and synagogues all over the country in retaliation. It
came to be known as the 'crystal night' because its
characteristic was the breaking of shop windows,
followed by widespread looting. In his Munich cabaret,
Weiss Ferdl appeared on the stage covered in jewellery.
The audience laughed. 'What's the matter?' he asked
them. 'Do you think I've been asleep during crystal
night?'
    A Jew, so one story went, keeps muttering something
as he walks along the street. A stormtrooper comes closer
and hears him say, 'Damn our Führer? Damn our
Führer!'
    'How dare you, you dirty Jew!' roars the Nazi.
    'But I don't mean *your* Führer,' explains the Jew, 'I
mean *ours*. If the fool hadn't led us out of Egypt, we might
now stand a chance of getting British nationality!'

The stormtroopers were kept busy marching and demonstrating to prop up the German people's morale, and there was a story about a deputation of SA men who go to see Hitler: could he not decree, they ask him, that now for a change they be allowed to tell jokes while the Jews do the marching?

'The weapon of criticism,' wrote Karl Marx, 'cannot replace the criticism by weapon.' This was evident as Germany entered her most violent and tragic era at the end of the 1930s. Clearly, the abundance of anti-Nazi jokes gave the lie to the claim of the rulers that 99 per cent of the people were behind them; but it took a World War, with many millions of casualties, immense destruction and the efforts of the most powerful nations to rid mankind of the vilest dictatorship of modern times. It would have been absurd to expect critical jokes to topple Hitler and his gang.

And yet: satire and sarcasm could have been the whispered expression of widespread antagonism to that dictatorship, promising popular support for an armed rising – if there had been one. As it turned out, active resistance was too sporadic, ill-organized and ill-timed to succeed. Had the high-ranking German officers who disagreed with the Nazi regime struck before or at the beginning of the war they might have carried the armed forces with them; but they attempted their *putsch* as late as 20 July 1944, when they saw that Germany would definitely lose the war; it failed disastrously. The conspirators, left without support, were caught and hanged from butchers' hooks. A year before, the students of the 'White Rose' movement who had tried to mobilize Germany's youth against the evil Nazi establishment had also been caught and beheaded. There was no general rising to rescue them from the executioner's axe – or to stop the mass deportations of Jews to the death camps.

During the war, underground jokes somewhat changed their character. The initial German victories in the West impressed popular opinion, though not nearly as much as the regime may have expected; after all, the German armies had stormed through Belgium and northern France in 1914 just as in 1940, and still the war had been lost. There were many jokes set in the German-occupied countries, but it is difficult to say whether they originated there or in Germany itself. One of the earliest stories of this kind concerned a Nazi officer being shown around Luxembourg by a local guide: 'And this,' explains the guide, 'is our admiralty.'

'Why do you need an admiralty?' asks the German. 'Luxembourg hasn't got a navy!'

'Is there not a Ministry of Justice in Berlin?' replies the Luxembourger.

This has become a recurrent joke; the Czechs told it in 1968 (the Russians ask Dubček why he has appointed a Minister of the Navy) and the Bolivians used it against the Chilean dictatorship in 1975.

The Dutch had their own anti-Nazi gags, such as raising their right arms and calling out, 'Heil Rembrandt!' When challenged by the Nazis they would say, 'Why shouldn't we hail one of our painters – don't you do it too?' In Paris, people told the story of Hitler's visit to Napoleon's tomb. He shouts down: 'Napoleon, before you stands the man who has accomplished what you failed to achieve – the conquest of Europe!'

From the depths of the tomb comes a voice: 'So you have conquered England too?'

'Not yet,' replied Hitler.

'Then climb down, brother, and lie beside me,' suggests the voice.

Picasso, according to another French story, is summoned by the Nazi commandant of Paris who shows him a reproduction of his famous painting of Guernica's destruction by German bombers in the Spanish civil war. 'Did you do that?' the commandant asks the artist in a menacing tone. 'No,' replies Picasso. 'You did.'

From Germany came the story about Hitler – who was superstitious and had his own astrologer-in-waiting –

arranging a spiritualist seance to call the spirit of Moses
into his presence. Moses duly appears.

'How did you manage to divide the waters of the Red
Sea?' asks Hitler. 'I should like to use the same method
for crossing the English Channel.'

'Well,' replied Moses, 'all I had to do was to touch the
waters with my magic rod.'

'And where can I find that rod now?' asks Hitler.

'In the British Museum,' chuckles the spirit of Moses.

In the later stages of the war the Dutch had a bitterly
satirical joke on the way the occupying Germans robbed
and starved Holland to feed themselves: a Dutchman
passes a railway siding where a herd of cows is being
driven into cattle trucks. He asks a railwayman what is
going on. 'Some unknown cow bit through a military
telephone wire,' is the answer, 'and now fifty cows are
being taken to Germany as hostages.'

In Norway they told the story of a local Quisling
supporter who is confronted by a resistance fighter:

'What are you going to do when Germany has lost the
war?'

'That's impossible,' says the collaborator. 'However, if
it should happen, then I'll just put on my hat and –'

'Put on your hat?' the patriot interrupts him. 'On
what?'

Listening to the BBC was, of course, strictly forbidden
in Germany and the German-occupied countries – but it
was done all the same, despite savage punishment if one
was caught. The German-language broadcasts from
London, listeners recalled after the war, did a marvellous
job by not only keeping the Germans informed about
what was really going on, but by propping up their faith
in the inevitable doom of the Nazi regime. Wisely, the
BBC entertained its listeners with a good deal of anti-Nazi
satire. The most popular speaker was 'Frau Wernicke', a
dry-witted Berliner, portrayed by a well-known German
cabaretist from the Weimar days, Annemarie Hase.
Among other humorous BBC series aimed at the
clandestine German listeners was one featuring a

disgruntled corporal writing to his wife, another was a comic dialogue between Munich citizens at the *Hofbräuhaus* beer cellar, and a third had a couple of front soldiers discussing the latest events.

A German woman, so the story goes, was brought into court in the winter of 1940–1, charged with listening to broadcasts from Britain. She defended herself quite innocently: 'We were told, weren't we, that the Führer would speak from London in October – I've been waiting for that ever since!'

During the last year of the war, another broadcasting station operated from Britain: the *Soldatensender*, pretending to be run by disaffected German soldiers somewhere in northern France. In fact it was a joint effort by the US Office of Strategic Services (OSS) and the British Political Intelligence Department (PID). Its accent was on caustic satire, much of it based on captured mail from and to German soldiers. The musical entertainment this radio station brought to its German listeners was something they had not been allowed to hear for a decade – jazz.

In Germany, jokes were turning sour during the last phase of the war. One which became almost proverbial had an optimist declaring, 'We're going to lose the war,' and a pessimist replying, 'Yes – but when?' Karl Valentin, so it was said, was doing duty as an air-raid warden on the roof of his Munich house, having heard the usual radio warning: 'An enemy squadron of bombers is flying towards the Munich area.' Valentin waited, scanning the sky; no enemy bombers were to be seen or heard. He scratched his head: 'I hope nothing's happened to them!'

His colleague, Weiss Ferdl, was said to have invested his money in paintings which eventually filled his whole flat. He stands before his latest acquisitions, the portraits of Hitler, Goebbels and Göring, and muses: 'Should one hang them or put them up against the wall?'

Old men and young boys were mobilized for the Home Guard, as a last-ditch defence of the fatherland. 'In the

Home Guard,' said the Germans, 'you get leave on two
occasions: for your confirmation and for your golden
wedding.' Official boasts about the enormous
effectiveness of the V1 and V2 bombs launched against
England in 1944–5 failed to impress the people. 'Now
we'll be getting the V3 as well,' they said. 'It's a rubber
boat that's going to circle the English coast until the
whole island is rubbed out' – a sarcastic allusion to
Hitler's boast of 1940: 'We shall rub out their cities!'

There was a general groan among the German soldiers
at the front: 'If we only had food like the English,
weapons like the Americans, Generals like the Russians –
and enemies such as the Italians!'

Italy, the country where Fascism was invented, is also the
traditional home of political wit – from Pompeian graffiti
and the jokes about the Vatican to pasquinades and quips
against Napoleon. Ridiculing Mussolini came quite
naturally to the Italian man-in-the-street, though active
resistance against the Fascists did not really suit his
temperament. This was confined to small groups of
Socialists and Communists, some of whom paid dearly
for their refusal to embrace the Duce's political religion.
Assassinations, torture by pumping castor oil into
dissidents' stomachs, and banishment to concentration
camps on lonely islands were characteristic of Fascist rule.

But Mussolini could not banish the jokes about his
braggadocio and delusions of grandeur, which spread
throughout Italy. Many stories were makeshift
modernizations of old ones that had been told about
former figures of fun such as Napoleon; others were
puns, a jocular form beloved by the Italians but difficult
to render in foreign languages. Still, some popular saws
and satirical stories can be understood by non-Italians,
such as: 'This is our beautiful liberty under Fascism –
everything that isn't prohibited is compulsory.' One
anecdote told of Mussolini's visit to a lunatic asylum

where the inmates are made to line up and welcome the great man. All of them cheer and raise their arms in the Fascist salute, except for a warden. An official of the Duce's entourage rebukes the man, and he replies, '*I'm not mad, am I?*'

The most favourite puns were about the *Foro Mussolini*, an old square in Rome that had been renamed in his honour. But *foro* means not only 'square', it also means 'hole'; thus one quip was, 'The *Foro Mussolini* is the last hole in our belt.' Other jokes about the square's new name referred, of course, to a certain hole in the human body.

Next to Mussolini, the most popular object of Italian political jokes was Starace, the Secretary of the Fascist Party. His stupidity and lack of education were proverbial; his only job at public events was that of announcing his master's appearance with the cast-iron phrase, '*Salutate il Duce, il fondatore del'Impero*' (Salute the Duce, the founder of the Empire). One day, according to a popular story, Starace's butler discovers a slip of paper with these words in the Party Secretary's pocket: he was too stupid to remember them by heart.

Two well-known Italians died in 1937: Marconi, the inventor of wireless telegraphy, and Musco, a famous Sicilian actor. 'Thank God,' said the Italians, 'it's the turn of the "M's" at last!' When prices rose sharply as a consequence of the costly war against the Abyssinians, a shopper asked his greengrocer how much the figs were:

'Three figs fifty lire,' said the greengrocer.

'Good heavens,' gasped the customer, 'how's that possible?'

'Well, sir, it isn't the figs that are worth so many lire; it's the lira that isn't worth a fig!' (An easily translatable pun, for 'fig' has the same double meaning in Italian as in English).

In the Spanish Civil War, too, Italian troops – called 'volunteers' – were sent by Mussolini to help his fellow-Fascist Franco. It was, of course, a rehearsal for the bigger war to come; apart from the Italians, the Germans were able to test their latest aircraft in aid of Franco, while the Republicans were helped by genuine volunteers in the International Brigade: Britons, Americans, Frenchmen and German anti-Hitler exiles. There was a sarcastic comment on the report that among some dozen casualties there had been one Spaniard: 'Serves him right – what business did he have to interfere?'

In Italy, there was much anger at the sacrifice of Italian lives for Franco. In order to divert people's attention, Mussolini now gave in to his friend Hitler's demand to take action against Italy's 50,000 Jews. When the Italian crack division was unable to break the Republican front at the Ebro, a question-and-answer joke circulated in Italy: 'Why has Mussolini suddenly begun to persecute the Jews?' Answer: 'Because he can't crush the Ebro; so he crushes the Ebreo (Jew) instead.'

Italy's airforce was much ridiculed because of its ineffectiveness and the bombastic claims made for it in official reports when it began to take part in Hitler's war. 'Ten of our aircraft raided Malta,' said a mock bulletin. 'Twelve of them returned safely.' A favourite saying was: 'Our Italian airmen are the most courageous in the world – they are the only ones who dare to fly Italian planes!' In Libya, Britain's General Wavell inflicted a humiliating defeat on Marshal Graziani; Mussolini dismissed him, and he was promptly dubbed 'Disgraziani' by the Italians.

A new maid, said a wartime story, is being engaged by a well-to-do Roman lady. The wage she is offered is not very generous:

'All right,' she says, 'but I want a bonus for keeping my mouth shut when you have insulted the Duce.'

'That won't help you much,' replies the lady. 'In this house the Duce is never insulted.'

'Well, then I want a bonus for keeping quiet about your supplies from the black market.'

'You're wrong again, we never buy on the black market.'

'Then I want a bribe for not informing the *Ovra* (secret

police) that you're listening to the Italian programme of the BBC.'

'We never listen to it.'

'Then I'm afraid this is no job for me,' says the girl. 'You don't criticize the Duce, you don't buy on the black market, you don't listen to the BBC – do you think I want to live with complete idiots?'

When Mussolini invaded Greece in 1940 (not for long, for the Greeks soon drove the Italians back to Albania where they had come from), bill-posters followed the troops and pasted Mussolini's picture on the walls of even the smallest villages. The posters were cut to ribbons almost as soon as they were put up. In one place the Italian commander imposed a fine of ten drachmas on every inhabitant 'for defacing the Duce's pictures' during the foregoing three weeks. The villagers lined up outside the commander's office, and the first to enter put twenty drachmas on the table. 'What does that mean?' asked the astonished Italian, and the man explained: 'We all want to pay the double fine right now, provided we're permitted to cut up your Duce for another three weeks!'

On the wall of a churchyard in Parma this inscription appeared shortly before the Allied landings in Italy: '*Fascisti, prenotate i posti!*' (Fascists, book your places in advance!); and a new *bon mot* was spreading through the country: 'The last thing an Italian wanted to be – in 1941, a soldier; in 1942, a Jew; in 1943, a Fascist.' The Sicilians, in a pessimistic mood, sighed: 'This is an unlucky island. First we got Fascism, then the Germans, and now these Allied bastards will probably land in Sardinia instead of here.'

When the Allies landed in North Africa, the Germans occupied southern France, and Italy also snatched a bit of it. Some Italian officers crowded into a French bus. 'Move forward, gentlemen,' the conductor told them. 'It'll be quite a change for you!'

Although the Italians were officially Nazi Germany's allies, they were in some respects treated by them as a conquered nation. Many Italians were brought to

Germany to work alongside the slave labourers from the occupied countries. Russian girls, too, had been deported to be employed as servants in German families. One of them, according to a story that was told in Berlin, consoled her mistress who was getting quite hysterical as the Russians were advancing on the town: 'Don't worry, Frau Maier. You haven't been treating me as badly as other German women treated their Russian maids. So when the Red Army comes I'll put in a word for you that they shouldn't torture you but shoot you right away.'

A good many war jokes were told in the Allied countries. One story made fun of the American lack of knowledge about the somewhat complicated European situation. In 1941, Secretary of State Cordell Hull informed President Roosevelt that Hungary had declared war on the United States:

Roosevelt: 'Tell the press that the Republic of Hungary ... and so on. By the way, what's the name of their president?'

Hull: 'Hungary is not a republic, it is a kingdom.'

Roosevelt: 'Is it? Who is the king?'

Hull: 'They haven't got one.'

Roosevelt: 'Then who is the Head of State?'

Hull: 'Vice-regent Admiral Horthy.'

Roosevelt: 'Have they got a fleet?'

Hull: 'No, Hungary has no coastline.'

Roosevelt: 'But why do they want to make war on us?'

Hull: 'Because we are now Russia's allies, and they want to fight Russia.'

Roosevelt: 'And why do they want to fight Russia?'

Hull: 'Because they want to get Transylvania.'

Roosevelt: 'Does that belong to Russia?'

Hull: 'No, to Roumania.'

Roosevelt: 'So why don't they fight the Roumanians?'

Hull: 'Because they are their allies ...'

In Britain, the presence of American soldiers as allies was not welcomed unanimously. Why not? Three reasons: They are overpaid, oversexed, and over here. Mrs Roosevelt, a good and courageous but not very beautiful woman, came to blacked-out England to see how her uniformed fellow-countrymen were doing. In Piccadilly Circus she runs into a drunken GI and shines her torch on him:

'My, that's a fine state you're in! Aren't you ashamed?'

The soldier shines his own torch on her.

'I'll be O.K. tomorrow, Missis,' he declares. 'But what about you?'

Among the various allies fighting shoulder to shoulder with the English were many refugees from Nazi Germany, the majority of them Jewish, who had been permitted to volunteer for the British army after having first been banned from any kind of employment in the United Kingdom and then interned as a potential fifth column in the event of Hitler's invasion of England. A number of them had joined the forces (initially, in fact, the Pioneer Corps) straight from the internment camps. They called the regiment to which they now belonged either 'The Kings Own Enemy Aliens' or 'The Hampstead Heath Highlanders'.

In 1943, the question of a 'Second Front', attacking the Germans in the West while the Russians were driving them back in the East, grew increasingly urgent. Churchill goes to Moscow to meet Stalin, so the story went, and finds a thirteen-year-old girl in his hotel bed. He protests in the Kremlin against this sort of thing. 'What's the worry?' says Stalin. 'You always take so long with your preparations. By the time you're ready she'll have come of age!'

While the Allies were still busy with the preparations for the Normandy landings, Stalin rang Churchill: 'Hallo, we're now here in Calais – do you still want us to wait?' In the same vein ran a 1944 'prediction' where the Allies would be found on Armistice Day: the Russians in Berlin, the Americans in Tokyo and the British at Monte Cassino.

When the war was over the Allies occupied their pre-arranged zones of Germany. Selected German families were allowed to invite American soldiers to their homes. One housewife is expecting the transatlantic guest allotted to her; the doorbell rings, and there stands a six-foot negro soldier. Unaccustomed to meeting non-Aryan people, she shrinks back:

'Haven't the authorities that sent you made some mistake?'

'Oh no,' says the black soldier. 'Colonel Levy never makes mistakes.'

4

Self-Criticism and Defence: The Jewish Joke

A great deal of material, from the scientific essay to the trivial jest book, has been published on the Jewish joke during the last one hundred years. Jewish wit and humour have grown to be almost proverbial, and the 'People of the Book' are often regarded as the People of the Joke.

Historically, however, this image is incorrect. The superficial assumption that the Jews, like some other Oriental peoples, were by nature endowed with a special sense of humour, with an inclination for inventing and telling funny stories, has no basis in ancient literature. The Bible, the oldest Jewish document, contains no humorous elements, although one finds an entertaining episode here and there. In contrast, for instance, to the orators and philosophers of ancient Greece who frequently used satire and sarcasm to make their points, the biblical prophets poured their rebuke and reproach with bitter scorn on the heads of their erring fellow-countrymen.

The Talmud, a great collection of Jewish books which includes the elaborations and interpretations of biblical laws and rules as well as many traditional stories, was begun during the Babylonian exile of the Jews in the sixth century BC. It became a basic work which helped to keep the Jews together as a tribal and religious entity after

their massive expulsion and exodus from Palestine. This
happened after AD 70 when the Romans conquered
Jerusalem, the capital of that rebellious people,
demolished their temple and dissolved their state. But the
Diaspora, which made tens of thousands of Jews seek new
homes all around the Mediterranean and right up to the
northern borders of the Roman Empire along the
Danube and the Rhine, did not annihilate Judaism. The
Talmud, which was constantly enlarged and refined by
the scholars until the sixth century AD, proved
indispensable as a spiritual bond among the now
far-flung Jewish settlements. This function of the
Talmud, regarded as most important by the rabbis, was
too serious to allow for the inclusion of light-hearted,
humorous material; there are even some passages about
people who put facetious questions to the scholars and
are firmly told off for their display of bad taste.

Admittedly, the earlier parts of the work contain some
jolly stories and anecdotes, but on closer inspection they
turn out to be Oriental tales of wise men and fools,
rascals and tricksters as they have always been told in the
Middle East: there is nothing particularly Jewish about
them.

Nor did the conditions under which the Jews had to live
in Central Europe during the first half of the Middle Ages
favour the development of a special kind of humour.
They were, at best, tolerated and had to accept any
restrictions imposed on them as they had nowhere else to
go. Cooped up in ghettos, forbidden to own land or to
practise any handicrafts (the Christian guilds were
organized on strict closed-shop principles), they were
reduced to a few branches of commerce. They had a
certain advantage, especially those living in sea ports, in
being able to trade with fellow Jews, friends or relatives in
other Jewish settlements: they knew and trusted one
another, which was more than most Christian merchants
could say about their foreign trading partners. Banks
were still unknown, so the Jews used the money they
earned by lending it to people with securities, last not

least to the princes who always needed cash. Inevitably, the Jews were called usurers.

Inevitably, they were held in contempt also as the people who had killed Jesus Christ – the Church saw to it that their collective and eternal guilt was never forgotten. It was most convenient to have these scapegoats handy for the slaughter. When there were epidemics, the Jews were charged with having poisoned the wells; when harvests failed, it was they who had put a curse on the land; when prices rose, they had made essential goods scarce. They were accused of barbaric secret rites, such as murdering Christian babies at their Passover ceremonies. So whenever it seemed expedient to the spiritual and temporal rulers, particularly in order to divert people's anger about the state of affairs, the ghettos were raided, the homes of the Jews looted, their places of worship burnt down and they themselves were beaten up, tortured or killed.

The crusades brought things to a head. Between the eleventh and thirteenth centuries, a number of major military expeditions to the Holy Land, then occupied by the 'infidel' Moslems, were organized by the Central and West European powers, originally to safeguard Christian pilgrims and then to conquer Palestine. There were also various other reasons for the crusades, political as well as social and commercial. While the knights set out for their adventures and their fight against the Saracens, the masses at home were whipped into senseless fury against the 'Saracens of Europe', the Jews. For all who had borrowed money from them – princes, merchants, squires, craftsmen – it was a splendid chance to get rid of their creditors.

England was no exception. Many Jews had settled there under William the Conqueror, and their lives had been comparatively peaceful. But in 1144, the calumny of a Christian boy's 'ritual murder' was used to start a general assault and slaughter of the Jews at Norwich. At the coronation of Richard I in 1189, a deputation of Jewish elders, trying to establish good relations with the

new King, went to Westminster where they were attacked
by the mob; the rumour was spread that the King had
ordered a general massacre of the Jews. In York, this
alleged royal command was carried out with particular
zeal. A hundred years later, all the Jews were expelled
from England, not to return until Cromwell invited them
back; some families from Holland were the first to accept
this invitation.

The most vicious persecution of the Jews came at the
very end of the Middle Ages in Spain, probably because
there they had achieved a magnificent symbiosis with the
Moors, the Islamic Arab invaders who had conquered
much of the country from the eighth century onwards
and who were driven out by the fifteenth. While keeping
their separate religious and cultural identities, the Arabs
and the Jews worked with each other in many fields,
particularly science, philosophy, the crafts and literature.
This cooperation of the two races, which laid the foun-
dations for a variety of later developments in the rest of
Europe, came to an end in 1492, the year Columbus
discovered America and the Arabs lost their last foothold
in Spain, Granada.

The Inquisition, established in 1478 by the Church as a
merciless system of suppression of heresies, was turned
against the Jews and the remnants of the Moslems in
Spain. Those who refused, even under torture, to
renounce their faith and become Christians were burnt
at the stake. A number of Jewish families managed to
escape to the Netherlands; others professed to accept the
Christian faith but secretly continued to practise Jewish
rites. The Spanish called them *marranos*, 'pigs'. By 1492,
no Jewish communities were left in the Iberian peninsula.

At that time, there were no more Jewish communities
in Central Europe either. The great exodus which had
begun with the first crusades was now complete. The
majority of the emigrants had gone to the
underpopulated countries of the East, to Poland, the
Ukraine and Lithuania, where they were at first
welcomed as settlers. Eventually, Russia's tsarist

authorities also allowed the Jews to settle. They gathered in the towns in certain quarters, partly for safety's sake, partly because the rulers of the host countries did not want them to mix with the rest of the population. Here, in these ghettos, Jewish culture and tradition survived; and here we may discover the first stirrings of 'Jewish wit'.

Of vital importance to the eastern Jewish immigrants was their language. Hebrew was holy to them and could therefore not be used in everyday life. What they spoke was Yiddish – basically, the medieval German they had brought with them. Still, many Hebrew terms (and some Hebrew syntax) were incorporated, and so were some Slavonic words; Yiddish is also written in Hebrew characters. It is a unique linguistic phenomenon because it has largely preserved a medieval idiom that has long ceased to exist in its homeland.

Yiddish developed its own literature and journalism in the nineteenth century, and the Jews took it with them on their further emigrations back to the West. Yet they were not always aware of the origins of their language, as this anecdote from the last century shows: Two Ukrainian Jews visit Berlin for the first time and hear, with some surprise, how the people speak there. 'These Germans,' says one of the visitors, 'are a funny lot. Fancy adopting our language and making such a hash of it!'

Their first few centuries in the East had brought the Jews some safety and modest prosperity. But then persecution started there as well. With the Cossack rebellions in the Ukraine in the seventeenth century, death and torture, rape and pillage came to the ghettos, and thereafter the Cossacks were used deliberately by the Russian authorities to harass the Jews. They were no longer safe in Poland, which was frequently under Russian occupation; the Swedes, the Prussians and later the Austrians joined the scrummage, each trying to annex a part for themselves – until Poland was brutally broken up and partitioned at the end of the eighteenth century.

After partition, most of the Jewish communities in
Poland came under the rule of the Russians, except for
those in the south who found themselves under the
Austrians. The latter kept the Jews under the thumb of a
corrupt and heartless bureaucracy, the former relegated
them to their age-old roles as scapegoats and milch cows.
Whenever the mood of the populace threatened to turn
against the tsarist establishment, there was always the
effective diversion of a 'pogrom', an organized attack on
the defenceless Jews.

Two hundred years ago, towards the end of the Age of
Enlightenment, there began a powerful movement
towards the emancipation of the Jews, meaning their
constitutional acceptance as full citizens, in the West. It
started in the new United States of America and
continued in revolutionary France; Germany followed in
the early nineteenth century and Britain in its second
half. Jewish families from Russian-dominated eastern
Europe began to emigrate to western Europe and
America in search of safety and liberty, and the trickle
grew into a flood as a result of the new wave of pogroms
which began in the 1880s.

However, the safety and liberty of the Jews all over the
European continent, after a century of great
contributions to the material and cultural development
of their host countries, proved in the end illusionary. The
National Socialists had incorporated in their programme
the elimination of the Jews from public life; eventually
they eliminated six million of them from life altogether.

What an unlikely people to develop a marked sense of
humour – except perhaps a kind of gallows-humour
after two thousand years of persecution, humiliation and
massacres! Yet resignation is precisely what Jewish wit
does not express. It has rather become a weapon of
criticism aimed by the Jews at their own faults and
less attractive traits; these have resulted from their
ambivalent situation, the consequence of their quandary

between oppression and emancipation, anti-Semitism and assimilation. It was this period between the late eighteenth and the early twentieth century which produced what we now recognize as Jewish humour, for it also produced the targets of Jewish self-criticism.

'The occurence of self-criticism,' wrote Freud (a life-long collector of Jewish jokes), 'may explain how it is that a number of the most apt jokes have grown up on the soil of Jewish popular life. They are stories created by Jews and directed against Jewish characteristics ... They know their real faults as well as the connection between them and their good qualities ... Incidentally, I do not know whether there are many other instances of a people making fun of its own character to such a degree.'

One of those foolish traits is the exaggerated anxiousness of many Jews not to create a bad impression among the *goyim*, the gentiles. A splendid example of self-criticism ridicules it: Two Jewish revolutionaries are to be executed by firing-squad. They are being tied to adjacent posts. Just before the final command is given, one of them calls out to the officer in charge, 'I want to be blindfolded!' 'Shshsh,' says the other, 'don't make trouble.'

Evidently, this is not the kind of joke created by anti-Semites to show Jews as figures of fun. Such 'Jewish jokes', or rather jokes about Jews, 'scarcely ever rise above the level of comic stories or of brutal derision', as Freud put it. They do not attack the real faults of their victims, but merely features of the image the anti-Semite likes to present of the Jew: a dirty, money-grabbing, egotistic and cunning rascal; above all, the fellow is a coward.

There is an interesting point here. Before the Diaspora as well as after the foundation of modern Israel two thousand years later, the Jews showed extraordinary courage and militancy fighting for their country. But in exile, they had no country to fight for, and one cannot blame them for being reluctant to risk their lives and limbs for Russia, Prussia or Austria at a time when these

countries denied them their simplest civil rights. In
contrast to the crude anti-Semitic jokes about cowardly
Jews, they had their own anti-militarist stories which
made their point of view clear. A rabbi, says one of them,
is being presented to the Emperor of Austria:

'Have you got any sons?' enquires the Emperor
affably.

'Thank God, yes,' replies the rabbi.

'Have they served in our army?', asks the Emperor.

'Thank God, no,' answers the rabbi.

The bourgeois Jews in Russia were civilians through
and through. One of them has been called up and sent to
the front. He climbs into the trench and says, 'Good day,
gentlemen, can you tell me the way to captivity?' A
Jewish soldier has been gravely wounded and lies in the
field hospital. A priest comes along on his routine tour
and holds up his cross to the man: 'Do you know what
this is, soldier?' The Jew grumbles, 'I'm lying here with a
bullet in my belly, and he asks me riddles!'

The Russian recruiting-sergeant combs a train for call-
up evaders. He finds an old Jew with a long white beard
hiding under a seat. 'Don't be ridiculous, old man,'
laughs the sergeant. 'You don't have to hide from me, at
your age!' 'And Generals you don't need?' asks the Jew.

Anti-Semitic jokes have always attacked the Jews'
materialism and overriding concern with their business.
But they themselves had the better stories; for instance:

An old Jew lies on his deathbed. 'Sarah, my wife, are
you here?' he asks.

'Yes, I'm here.'

'Nathan, my son, are you here?'

'Yes, father.'

'Esther, my daughter, are you also here?'

'Yes, father, I'm here.'

'And who's minding the shop?'

A popular nineteenth-century story (borrowed and
christianized, by the way, by Somerset Maugham) tells of
a Jew from the ghetto of Krotoszyn in Poland who applies
for the position of a *shammes*, a humble synagogue

servant. 'Can you read and write?' the rabbi asks him. He cannot, and is turned down. Unable to find another job he emigrates to western Europe: he starts with a market stand, moves into a shop, acquires a few more shops, then a factory, and ends up a business tycoon. His biggest rival, a Christian, suggests a merger between their commercial empires. The deal comes off, the documents are ready for signature.The Christian signs, but the Jew makes only three crosses. The Christian is amazed:

'So you are illiterate? Good heavens, a man with your enormous gifts – what would have become of you if you could read and write?'

'I can tell you exactly,' replies the Jew. '*Shammes* in Krotoszyn.'

In recent years, the Yiddish–Hebrew word *chutzpah*, roughly translatable as 'impertinence' or 'cheek', has been adopted by English writers and journalists. The Jews themselves use it as a term of disapproval of a common Jewish fault. Famous for their *chutzpah* were the matchmakers, an essential profession in Jewish communities in the old days; no marriage was thinkable without their part in bringing bride and bridegroom together.

A matchmaker goes to a rich Jew and tells him that he has an eminently suitable girl for his son:

'I don't interfere in my son's affairs,' says the rich man.

'Ah, but you don't know who the girl is,' says the matchmaker. 'She's the daughter of Baron Rothschild!'

'Well, in that case ...'

The matchmaker then goes to Rothschild:

'I have a splendid man for your daughter,' he says.

'You're wasting your time. My girl will be choosing her fiancé only among the top circles.'

'Ah, but you don't know who the man is. He's the vice-president of the International Bank.'

'Well, in that case ...'

Now the matchmaker visits the President of the International Bank:

'I have a wonderful vice-president for you,' he says.

'But I have already two vice-presidents,' replies the great banker.

'Ah, but you don't know who the man is,' says the matchmaker. 'He's the future son-in-law of Baron Rothschild!'

The story was also told in Israel in the 1970s to characterize the diplomatic efforts of Dr Henry Kissinger, then US Secretary of State, to bring peace to the Middle East.

But there is also a Jewish kind of modesty which the Jews themselves like to satirize. Typical is this story: The squire advertises for a tutor for his children, and a little old Jew turns up.

'Well,' says the squire, 'I was actually thinking of someone younger than you. But I suppose you have the required qualifications. Are you good at history?'

'Not really, sir.'

'What about geography?' asks the squire.

'Well, I must confess –'

'Calligraphy?'

'Calli ... What's that?'

The squire gets rather annoyed with the man:

'What the hell did you come here for?'

The Jew explains, 'Sir, I just wanted to tell you that you shouldn't rely on me for the job.'

Combining the material joys of life with other, more spiritual elements has often been looked upon by the Jews as a Jewish fault. Yet perhaps things are not as simple as that. One of the most moving stories by Heinrich Heine goes down to the very roots of traditional Jewish attitudes. In his *Baths of Lucca*, written in 1829, he has a magnificent comic character, a little Jewish lottery collector from Hamburg who philosophizes about religion:

There lives a man in Hamburg by the name of Moses Lump; they call him Lumpy for short. He runs around the whole week in wind and rain with his pack on his back to earn a few marks. But when he comes home on a Friday night he finds the seven-armed candelabrum lit, there's a white cloth on the table, and he puts down his pack and his worries and sits down at the table with his lopsided wife and his even more lopsided daughter, eats with them fish cooked in a delicious white garlic sauce, sings the most beautiful songs of King David, rejoices with all his heart at the exodus of the Children of Israel from Egypt, rejoices also that all the villains who did evil to them died eventually, that King Pharaoh, Nebuchadnezzar, Haman, Antioch, Titus and all those people are dead while Lumpy is still alive and eats fish with his wife and child – and I tell you, Herr Doctor, the fish is exquisite and the man is happy, he doesn't have to worry about education, he sits in his religion and in his green dressing-gown as merrily as Diogenes in his tub, he looks merrily at his candles which he doesn't even have to trim himself – and I tell you, if they burn a little dim and the *shabbes* woman who ought to trim them isn't at hand, and the great Rothschild happens to drop in with all his brokers, accountants, shipping clerks, and *chefs de comptoir* with whom he has conquered the world, and if Rothschild would say: 'Moses Lump, ask what you like, and it shall be done' – Herr Doctor, I am convinced Moses Lump would reply quietly: 'Trim the candles for me!' and the great Rothschild would say in amazement, 'If I wasn't Rothschild, I'd like to be such a Lumpy!'

The Jews' self-criticism is the unmistakable sign that they have a highly developed sense of humour, for without it you cannot laugh at your own failings. However, the greater part of traditional Jewish jokes are ghetto jokes about characters and situations in their tightly-knit communities: about rich and poor men, marriage and business, clever *shnorrers* and pompous rabbis, doctors and crooks. Yiddish literature deals largely with such people, and some anecdotes from oral tradition – Jews are great story-tellers – have found their way into other countries and languages. For instance, the French have a popular old music-hall song, '*Tout va très bien, Madame la Marquise*', which originates in a classic Jewish tale:

A man from Pinne in Poland returns after a long journey and asks a friend about the latest news in town.

'There isn't much,' replies the friend. 'A little dog barked.'

'A dog barked, is that all?'

'Well, there was such a crowd, and someone must have stepped on its tail.'

'Why?' asks the man from Pinne.

'No particular reason, except some kind of brawl.'

'A brawl? Who was involved?'

'Your brother, as a matter of fact. A policeman hit him, and he hit back,' says the friend.

'My brother? Why did the policeman hit him?'

'Because he resisted arrest.'

'My brother arrested? What for?'

'Well, it seems he forged some cheques.'

'He has forged cheques? But he's been doing that for ages!'

'I told you, there's nothing new in Pinne,' replies the friend.

Several variations on that theme have been current; one says that the crowd had gathered because the house of the man who returned was on fire, another that his wife ran away with a lover; but the beginning and end are always the same. A harmless story, reflecting some aspects of Jewish small-town life.

But what about the defence of the Jews, by satire, against the pressures of a hostile outside world? Strangely enough, there is very little that could be called resistance to anti-Semitism; somehow, the hopelessness of making an impression, by the weapon of wit, on a fanatical enemy may have silenced the jokers. As Henri Bergson declared, laughter is always the laughter of a group, an expression of complicity with other laughers. But in a world where a small Jewish minority would not expect to find many sympathizers among the rest of the population, the laughers were only other Jews – and what would have been the point of an anti-anti-Semitic joke that would never hit the target?

Still, there were a small number of jokes trying to ridicule the enemy. The simplest, and even today the most popular of them, is this dialogue:

'It's all the fault of the Jews,' says the anti-Semite.

'And of the cyclists,' replies the Jew.

'Why the cyclists?'

'Why the Jews?' asks the Jew.

Other dialogues between Jews and their detractors originated at a time when the Prussian Lieutenant was the most typical of the latter. Then there were school jokes about 'little Moritz' (a typical eastern Jewish boy's name), showing him as the most quick-witted pupil amongst his Christian class-mates. But the great majority of 'defensive' Jewish jokes were aggressive ones, aimed at the deserters – Jews who got themselves baptized in the hope of easier careers, promotion and acceptance by Christian society. The stories about them, which all make fun of the futility of their efforts, sprang up in Central Europe during the Wilhelminian and late Habsburg era when baptism was regarded as the ultimate form of assimilation; the racialist philosophy – 'A Jew is a Jew is a Jew' – propagated by Richard Wagner's English-born son-in-law, Houston Stewart Chamberlain, was then still in its embryonic phase.

The general feeling among the Jewish bourgeoisie towards those deserters was that one does not escape from a beleaguered fortress. Sarcasm was the keynote of most of the jokes about them. A Jewish lawyer, about to be baptized, asks a Christian colleague what one wears on such an occasion. 'That's a difficult question,' is the answer. 'You see, what *we* wear are nappies.' Sometimes baptism goes wrong: one anecdote tells about a rich Jew who travels to Rome for the purpose: 'Three cardinals got busy on the job, but they had to give up in despair.' At the other end of the social scale, a small-town insurance agent goes to the local parson to get baptized.

After several hours he returns home, bathed in sweat.

'It was terrible,' he confesses.

'But you are baptized now, aren't you?' ask the family.

'No,' he answers. 'But the parson is insured.'

A typical figure of fun and the heroine of many stories was 'Frau von Pollak', wife of a Polish–Jewish upstart, baptized and ennobled (for a substantial donation) by the German or Austrian establishment. She tries desperately to disguise her origins. One story describes her first confinement: Herr von Pollak has secured the services of Berlin's top-ranking obstetrician for the occasion, and they both wait outside madame's bedroom for the moment of action.

'*Oh, mon dieu, que je souffre!*' they hear her exclaim.

'Please, doctor, go in,' says Herr von Pollak.

'Not yet,' replies the obstetrician.

Some time later, madame calls out in her most educated German, '*Ach Jesus, diese Schmerzen!*' and her worried husband urges the doctor, 'High time – please hurry!'

'Not yet,' the doctor smiles calmly.

But when madame cries out at last, '*Oi mamme!*' in her native Yiddish, he says, 'That's it,' and goes to deliver the baby.

Some defensive Jewish jokes were aimed, directly or indirectly, at the primitive 'collective guilt' doctrine of the Christians that 'the Jews killed our Lord'. There are some poignant stories, usually in dialogue form:

'I have been forbidden to play with you,' says a Christian girl to little Moritz. 'My parents say you Jews have crucified Jesus!'

'Not us,' he protests. 'That must have been the Cohens next door.'

Another dialogue is this one:

'My son has been accepted at the seminary,' a proud Christian father tells a Jewish friend.

'And what for?' asks the Jew.

'He'll become a priest.'

'And then?'

'Oh, one day he may rise to be a bishop or even a cardinal,' says the Christian father.

'And then?'

'Above the cardinal there's only His Holiness the Pope.'

'I see. And what then?' continues the Jew.

'Don't be stupid. Above the Pope there's only our Lord.'

'Well,' says the Jew, 'one of our boys made it.'

Shapiro's son has been baptized, and the rabbi reproaches him for not having prevented the young man from taking such a step.

'What will you say to the Almighty when he asks you how you could tolerate this?' asks the rabbi.

'I shall reply: and what about your son?' says Shapiro.

Heinrich Heine also became a Christian. When he was on his death-bed, his wife said she was praying that God would forgive him. 'He will,' said Heine. 'After all, that's his job.'

Perhaps the most impudent Jewish story – some Christians might even call it blasphemous – is of comparatively recent origin:

The Pope has died and goes to heaven. St Peter asks him whom among the saints he would like to meet.

'Saint Mary, the mother of Jesus Christ,' says the Pope.

Peter leads him into a palatial hall. There, in a far corner, sits an old Jewish lady. The Pope approaches her reverently and sinks to his knees.

'O Holy Mother of God,' he says, 'all my life on earth I have been looking forward to this blessed moment. There is one question I want to ask you – what was it like to give birth to our Lord Jesus Christ?'

The old Jewish lady wags her head and smiles: 'Vell, ectually ve vonted a little girl ...'

Zionism, the concept of the Jews' return to their ancient homeland Palestine, was by no means a welcome movement among the German Jews who, under the

Kaiser and even more in the Weimar Republic, believed they were well on the road to complete assimilation and genuine equality. 'When we have our own state in Palestine,' was an often-heard quip, 'I'd like to be Jewish ambassador in Berlin.' The idea of moving from comfortable, well-organized Central Europe to the wilds of the Middle East did not appeal very much to the Jewish bourgeoisie. 'A Zionist,' went one of their favourite *bons mots*, 'is a Jew who sends another Jew to Palestine at the expense of a third Jew.'

Theodor Herzl himself, the founder of Zionism – he was the correspondent of a Viennese newspaper covering the Dreyfus trial in France when the idea occurred to him – had some initial doubts whether Palestine, then part of the Turkish Empire, was a suitable area for a modern Jewish state. However, there was no prospect of gaining much Jewish support for emigration to any country except the land of the Bible. Even among the East European Jews, with their more orthodox tradition, Zionism met with some resistance because, according to religious belief, the Jews would return to their ancient homeland only when the Messiah had appeared to lead them there and establish a new age of peace and prosperity. To the orthodox rabbis, therefore, Zionism was a sacrilege.

Only as the tide of Nazism began to rise did the movement gain popularity, particularly among Jewish youth. But there were many jokes reflecting the reluctance of the older generation to settle in Israel, as the new state was to be called. 'Dear God,' sighs an immigrant, 'for two thousand years we've been praying in vain for our return – and now it has to happen to me, of all people!'

Even the prospect of living among fellow-believers does not seem to have appealed to many Jews. Freud, in his book on the joke, tells a story that criticizes a certain side of the Jewish character which had little attraction to westernized Jews – over-familiarity. A Galician Jew is travelling by train on a hot day. Being alone in his compartment, he makes himself comfortable, taking off his jacket and tie, rolling up his sleeves and putting his feet on the opposite seat. Another traveller enters, well-dressed and well-mannered, obviously a *goy*. The Galician at once takes his feet off the seat, rolls down his sleeves and puts on his tie and jacket. The gentleman thumbs his diary and suddenly turns to the Galician:

'Excuse me, do you happen to know when we have Yom Kippur?' he asks.

'Oi so,' says the Galician, taking off his jacket and making himself comfortable again. He feels that for a fellow-Jew he does not have to behave himself.

Early Israeli jokes harp on some traditional characteristics of the Jews which, in fact, soon disappeared in the new community. A storm is about to break as an Israeli liner weighs anchor, and an anxious passenger appears on the bridge: 'Captain, one doesn't travel in such weather!' The new army, too, came in for some old-fashioned fun: A soldier passes an officer in the street without saluting.

'You there,' the officer shouts, 'why don't you salute me?'

'Sorry, sir, I didn't see you,' replies the soldier.

'Oh good,' says the officer, 'that's all right then. I was afraid you had something against me.'

It was to be expected that the Jews in Israel would use their sense of humour for political criticism in their own state; although there is no authoritarian restriction of public opinion, the pressures of everyday life in a condition of siege, in a country with the most serious political and economic problems, need the safety-valve of satirical jokes. A classic Israeli story is that of a secret session of the Cabinet:

'I would like to suggest a very good solution for our troubles,' says the Minister of Finance. 'All we have to do is to declare war on America.'

'But that's madness,' says the Prime Minister. 'Of course we'd lose that war.'

'Sure we will, and then all our problems will be solved.

Remember post-war Germany!' replies the Minister of Finance.

'I think it's too risky,' says the Minister of Defence. 'What if we win?'

One minister has innumerable children – a constant source of jokes for the Israelis. When one of his boys comes home incredibly dirty, the minister asks his wife, 'Shall we wash him or make a new one?'

Israel's future may remain one big question mark. But then, this symbol has been hanging over the Jews for two thousand years. There is a rather sad 'joke' which sums up that people's attitude and perhaps offers one reason why they have survived; it was told, probably not for the first time, in the Balkans in 1942 when the German invasion was imminent, and it turned up again, brought up to date, in Israel in the late 1970s:

A Christian priest, a Moslem imam, and a rabbi discuss what they would do if another Great Flood were about to sweep over the earth.

'We would pray that God may spare us,' says the priest.

'We would accept our fate as kismet and die in resignation,' says the imam.

But the rabbi says: 'We would learn to live under water.'

5

Jokes from the East

There is no doubt that the humour of the Jews in Russia was strongly influenced by that of the Russians themselves, with their tradition of satirical literature and verbal jokes. Both Jews and Russians derived much of their humour from their social and political situation, particularly in the last century; most of them were living in poverty, they had to endure injustice, their public and personal liberties were almost non-existent. Laughter was the great relief, but it was 'laughter under invisible tears', as Gogol described it.

The verbal joke flourished among both peoples, though not for the same reasons. Literacy is an obligatory element of Jewish education, but among the orthodox ghetto communities this meant literacy in Hebrew, the language of the holy books and of prayer. Yiddish was the everyday idiom; knowledge of the host people's language was acquired only casually and merely for practical purposes. Thus there was among the East European Jews no massive reading public for books and journals in Russian, Polish, Ukrainian or Lithuanian, while Yiddish literature developed – because of lack of money and of technical facilities – only in the second half of the last century. Thus Jewish humour in the East expressed itself mainly in verbal form. And so did popular Russian humour – for a very simple reason: until the 1917 Revolution, over 80 per cent of the people were illiterate, and even today the standard of literacy in the Soviet

Union is still somewhat below that of the West European countries.

The educated Russian bourgeoisie had, of course, its theatres, and since they played to only a tiny minority the censors did not suppress the satirical comedies that were greatly in favour with the intelligentsia – Gogol's *Government Inspector* (1836), for instance, which is one of the classics of dramatic satire. However, the editors and contributors of the numerous satirical journals published since the late eighteenth century – with titles such as *The Money Bag*, *The Drone*, *The Busy Bee*, *Satirical News*, *Observer on the Neva* – often got into trouble with the authorities because of their sharp political and social criticism. Some of these people landed in Siberia, and a few who took part in the Dekabrist rebellion of 1825 were executed.

During the first ten years of the Soviet Union there was great enthusiasm among Russian writers and artists for the Revolution and for the liberty it promised. It seemed as if satire and humorous criticism would become a permanent feature of Soviet life. There was Mikhail Soshchenko, who specialized in making fun of the difficulties and absurdities of the evolving new society, satirizing bureaucrats and bone-headed citizens; his short-stories and novels (e.g., *Sleep Faster, Comrade*) were translated into several western languages. The writers' team of Ilf and Petrov produced a humorous novel which also made the grade in international literature: *The Twelve Chairs*, the story of a treasure hunt across Russia; survivors of the propertied classes, Party *apparatchiks*, Muscovites and provincials, crooks and priests – all come under the authors' satirical fire. In their joint autobiography, Ilf and Petrov wrote: 'It is very difficult to write together. We are not even related to each other; we come from different backgrounds – one of us is a Russian (the enigmatic Russian soul), the other a Jew (the enigmatic Jewish soul).' The novel was published in the late 1920s at the end of Lenin's 'New Economic Policy' (NEP), launched as a means to liberalize trade and production, and so make life easier for a society that was dragging its feet on the road to Communism.

Ilya Ehrenburg, the Jewish writer, emigrated from revolutionary Russia to Paris, where he stayed until his return when Nazi Germany attacked the Soviet Union in 1941. In Paris he wrote one of the few picaresque novels of modern literature, the delightful *Stormy Life of Lazar Roitshvantz*. The hero is a little Jewish ghetto tailor whose dramatic adventures take him through half a dozen countries and twenty prisons; he tries his hand at innumerable jobs – rabbit breeder in Tula, rabbi in Frankfurt, police informer for Scotland Yard, film actor in Berlin, pioneer in Palestine, painter in Paris. Lazar's literary soulmates are Voltaire's Candide as well as Shveyk. Ehrenburg castigates the NEP spivs in Russia, the phoney artists of the Quartier Latin, the speculators in the Weimar Republic. It is a very funny yet truthful canvas of the inter-war world.

In 1922, Soviet Russia got its famous satirical weekly, *Crocodile*, a name taken from traditional children's tales in which that reptile appears in human clothes, fearsome but friendly and resourceful. Right from the start, the journal was·meant to use the 'weapon of criticism' against official stupidities and abuses, acting as a reminder of what the Socialist society was all about. But things changed for *Crocodile*, as they did for all humorous writing in the Soviet Union, when Lenin died and Stalin emerged as the new dictator, Trotsky being expelled from Russia and the NEP called off. Significantly, *Crocodile* was taken over by *Pravda*, the organ of the Communist Party; ever since, it has had to redirect its satirical arrows at capitalist countries, with only a small number of harmless digs at the imperfections of Soviet man. The country's genuine satire was left to the people who made and spread Russia's political jokes; there has never been any lack of them.

The conversation of the two friends at the Kremlin wall, with which this book begins, was one of the many jokes of the early post-revolutionary years. The Russian Jews, who were now scarcely better off than in tsarist days – despite the large number of Jewish intellectuals among the revolutionary leaders – had their own sad and sarcastic way of commenting on the situation: A Jewish citizen, reduced to beggary by the revolution, has died of starvation; he takes his empty pouch up to heaven, dumps it at the feet of Karl Marx and tells him, 'Here's the interest of your *Kapital*!'

Another story was very popular among the Jews who, around 1920, were looking in vain for signs that the traditional Russian anti-Semitism had gone for ever. The scene is a tramcar in a provincial town. 'Lenin Square,' announces the conductor. 'Formerly Nicholas Square,' mutters a Jewish passenger. The conductor gives him a warning look as he calls out, 'Street of the October Revolution,' whereupon the Jew says under his breath, 'Formerly Street of Peter the Great.' Now the conductor gets really annoyed and shouts, 'Hold your tongue, Comrade Israelite!' 'Formerly dirty Jew,' comments the passenger.

Quite inter-denominational was a jocular question-and-answer that made the rounds in those lean years: 'What was the nationality of Adam and Eve?' 'They must have been Russians because they had no clothes, no roof over their heads, and only one apple between them – yet they insisted they were living in Paradise.' Jokes about shortages were then more abundant than food and consumer goods. 'We are now marching towards Communism; but why don't we get enough food?' was a popular question. The answer: 'One does not eat while marching.' What are the critical seasons in Soviet agriculture? ran another question; the answer: spring, summer, autumn and winter.

'I've just ordered a twelve-piece bedroom suite for my family, directly from Leningrad,' a Muscovite tells his friend, who is duly impressed.

'Twelve pieces? Marvellous!'

'Yes: eleven bags of straw and one picture of Lenin.'

It was said that Nicholas Bukharin, the Communist theoretician and editor of *Izvestia*, was the author of this story about Lenin, whom he had known intimately: Lenin has died and appears at St Peter's gate. He is admitted on trial, and St Peter is told to keep an eye on him. After a week or so, God asks him, 'Well, Peter, how's Lenin's re-education progressing?' 'Fine, Comrade God,' answers St Peter. Bukharin's sense of humour does not seem to have been approved by Stalin, however, for he was executed after a show trial in 1938.

Among the trouble-makers under Stalin's rule was Krupskaya, the widow of Lenin, but even Stalin could not afford to have her 'liquidated'. He summons her, according to one story, and threatens, 'If you don't stop criticizing me, I'll have someone else appointed Lenin's widow!'

Stalin died in 1953, and three years later Khrushchov, his successor, denounced and debunked him in his famous speech at the Twentieth Congress of the Communist Party. Now Stalin's body could no longer be allowed to lie in state beside that of Lenin in the mausoleum on Moscow's Red Square. Perhaps, some Russian officials were said to have asked, Stalin's remains could be shipped to Palestine and re-interred there? 'Oh no,' replied the Israeli Prime Minister, Ben Gurion, to Moscow's inquiry, 'we've already had one resurrection here!'

Stalin's dethronement posed a major problem for the Soviet historians. They had already eliminated Trotsky from their books – but how should they handle Stalin's biography? 'It's hard for them to predict the past accurately,' quipped the Russians.

Khrushchov had a rustic Ukrainian sense of humour, and he probably did not mind this anecdote when he heard it around 1960: He had visited Paris and decided to open a French-style brothel in Moscow as an official institution. It was no success, and when a French diplomat visited Khrushchov he complained, 'I don't understand where we went wrong. It can't be the fault of the girls – they are the most trustworthy specimens we could find, all of them Party members since 1917!'

He invited his mother, a simple peasant woman, to Moscow to show her how he was living as the country's top official. She tiptoed through his thickly-carpeted, magnificent residence; they rode in a luxury limousine, driven by a uniformed chauffeur, to his splendid *dacha*. The old woman was overawed but a little worried. 'Nikita,' she said, 'what are you going to do if the Reds come back?'

When Khrushchov was deposed in 1965, Brezhnev succeeded him. Jokes about this dour, conservative man soon began to circulate in Russia. An early one had him hijacked in mid-Atlantic in his Aeroflot jet. 'Send us one million roubles in dollar notes,' the hijackers asked the Soviet government by radio, 'or we send him back!'

Brezhnev, according to a later anecdote, opens a meeting of the Politburo, the ruling body of the Party, with a stern warning about leaks from its sessions. No member is allowed to leave the room all day, he declares. After some hours of discussions, one member asks to be allowed to fetch an important file from his office. Brezhnev refuses to let him go. An hour or so later, there is a knock on the door: a KGB official appears with that file.

'How did you know it was required?' asks Brezhnev. 'We heard it on the BBC,' replies the KGB man.

'Floating shortages,' meaning the scarcity or disappearance of this or that food item, have remained a feature of Soviet life. A customer comes into a large food store and asks at a counter, 'Have you got any caviar?' 'Sorry,' says the assistant, 'we are the department where there is no meat. Over there is the department where they haven't got any caviar.'

The most permanent shortage, however, is that of homes; but it is common knowledge that you can get one if you make friends with the right people. A young woman has been on the housing list for a long time without getting a flat. In the end she succeeds in making

her way to the ante-room of the boss of the local housing
department, and asks to see him. The secretary has strict
orders not to admit petitioners. So the young woman
writes a note, puts it in an envelope and tells the secretary
to take it to her boss. The note reads:

'Dear Comrade Ivan Sergeyevitch, I should like to see
you personally. After all, didn't we sleep together only a
fortnight ago?'

At once she is admitted to the boss, who promises to
put her right at the top of the housing list. Then he looks
at her pensively:

'Excuse me, comrade, I'm trying to recall that occasion
when we were supposed to have slept together.'

'But don't you remember – it was the week before last
at our local Party meeting!'

When the Russians and the Chinese began to quarrel,
popular humour in the Soviet Union made its own acid
comments, for instance: Moscow has installed a super-
computer which can predict the future. The Kremlin
men ask the machine what will happen in the year 2000.
'Nothing important,' replies the computer. 'All quiet on
the Chinese–Finnish front.' Another joke on the same
subject: Brezhnev's secretary comes to the leader and
reports, 'Comrade Leonid Ilyitch, I have some news. First
the bad news: the Chinese have landed on the moon.
Now the good news: all of them!' (Some years later, the
Czechs had their own version of this story – it was the
Russians who were said to have landed on the moon, and
the hopeful reply was, 'All of them?')

One story, anticipating Brezhnev's death, tells of a
meeting between him and Nicholas II, last of the tsars, in
the nether regions of the beyond:

'Tell me,' asks the Tsar, 'is Holy Russia still a Great
Power?'

'Certainly,' replies Brezhnev.

'And has it still got a big army?'

'It has.'

'And does it still stretch from the Baltic to the Pacific?'

'It does.'

'And do the secret police hold the people in their grip?'

'Yes.'

'And do my people still drink vodka?'

'They do.'

'Is it still 38 per cent proof?'

'Oh no, it's 40 per cent today,' says Brezhnev.

'Now tell me one thing,' Nicholas asks finally, 'was it really necessary to make a revolution for a mere two per cent?'

Yerevan is the capital of Soviet Armenia, and its economic and cultural centre; it has, of course, a state-controlled radio transmitter. But there is also a fictitious station called Radio Yerevan (or Eriwan); one wonders if the name of the non-existant station is a hint at Samuel Butler's utopian satire set in the land of Erewhon ('Nowhere' spelt backwards). The station is famous throughout Russia and the whole bloc of 'People's Republics' in eastern Europe as a font of popular humour and as a peg on which to hang all kinds of critical jokes. Radio Yerevan's 'question hour' is their usual framework; the answers begin, as a rule, with the words 'Basically yes (or no), but ...'

'Is it true that the Americans have more cars than we in Russia?', a 'listener' wants to know. Yerevan's answer: 'Basically yes, but we've got much more parking space.'

Question: 'Is there a real chance of friendship with the Germans?'

Answer: 'Basically yes. They seem to have forgiven us for their attack on the Soviet Union.'

Question: 'Would it be beneficial for West Germany to change over from capitalism to Socialism?'

Answer: 'Basically yes, but what a pity – all that splendid industry!'

Question: 'Is it legally permitted to demonstrate in the Soviet Union?'

Answer: 'Basically yes. We are being informed that the

square in front of the Chinese Embassy in Moscow will be greatly enlarged for the purpose.'

A listener complains: 'I ordered a steak at the Samovar restaurant in Moscow, but although their meat is known to be the best in town and their knives are always sharp, I couldn't cut it. Can you explain that?'

Answer: 'Basically no, but perhaps you've hit a microphone inside?'

Another listener wants to know what the latest regulations on civil defence recommend in case of a nuclear attack.

Answer: 'Take a sheet, wrap it around yourself, and walk to the nearest cemetery.'

Sex is more or less taboo in the Soviet and satellite press: all the more reason why Radio Yerevan makes it the subject of a good many questions. For instance:

'When I came home from the factory last night, I found my wife in bed with another man. How can I prevent that happening again?'

Answer: 'Work more overtime.'

Question: 'Is prostitution permitted in the Soviet Union?'

Answer: 'Basically no, but if you have any addresses, send them to us.'

Question: 'Are Soviet men faithful when they go on official trips?'

Answer: 'Basically yes, especially our astronauts.'

Question: 'Is it permitted to have sex in public on the Red Square in Moscow?'

Answer: 'Basically yes. But you must be prepared to accept the militia's official advice and guidance.'

Occasionally, the station makes a non-political sex joke: 'Can a couple of homosexual men produce a baby?'

Answer: 'Basically no, but they keep trying.'

Some Yerevan jokes are distinctly sour:

Question: 'Why are your programmes so difficult to receive?'

Answer: 'Because we broadcast from Siberia.'

Another listener wants to know whether the station would send its replies by post. The answer: 'Basically yes. But who would tell us his address?'

Radio Yerevan starts a competition for the best political joke. First prize: twenty years in a labour camp.

You can nearly always tell whether a joke has originated on the eastern or the western side of the Iron Curtain. But there is at least one that might have come either from Russia or from England: A Soviet trade-unionist visits Britain and boasts to his English opposite number about labour relations in Russia: 'Our happy workers never complain, never ask for higher wages, never work to rule or go on strike.' The Englishman shakes his head sadly. 'You'll never get those conditions in our country, mate,' he says. 'This lot are all bleeding Communists!'

Poland has always been the victim of geography. Hemmed in, invaded and divided by the aggressive empires that grew up around it, Poland needed extraordinary faith and will-power on the part of its people to stay alive at all. Their gallows-humour reacted sarcastically to each new disaster. 'Poor Poland,' they said as the country was partitioned no fewer than three times at the end of the eighteenth century, 'God is too high above, and France too far away.' That nation was traditionally Poland's only friend among the European powers, but Napoleon's defeat in Russia also meant that the Poles lost what was left of their independence, and their country became a province of the Tsar's empire. Only Russia's defeat in the First World War and the Russian revolution gave Poland its freedom back.

After the Second World War, history and geography imposed on the Poles a new form of control: Stalinist Russia in the east, the Communist German Democratic Republic in the west and hostile Czechoslovakia in the south – they all had a vested interest in keeping Poland a docile member of the Eastern bloc.

But this is exactly what the Poles hate to be. Their mental make-up, their intellectual and cultural tendencies, and above all their Roman Catholicism have made them the most westernized nation in that part of the world. Sad historical experience has imbued them with a fierce love of their tortured country, and their temperament endowed them with a *courage fou* which made them, in 1939, attack the invading tanks of Nazi Germany with their old-fashioned cavalry. It is the same courage which often prompts them to oppose unpopular decrees by popular force – unheard of in any other Communist country. Twice, in 1956 and 1970, they succeeded even in bringing down the government, thus stopping the threatened rise in food prices (as they had already stopped the attempt to impose agricultural collectives). All this was in the face of Soviet pressure which might well have resulted in a military invasion of their obstinate country.

On the whole, the Polish people are well aware of the never-ending problems with which their government has to cope; after all, their ministers are also Poles with the same likes and dislikes as the rest of the population. The Catholic Church, which is particularly strong among the peasants, acts as an efficient counterbalance to the Communist Party. There was a certain danger that the enthusiastic welcome for the first Polish-born Pope, John Paul II, on his visit to his homeland in 1979 might provoke the country's neighbours to some kind of action; they must have grown rather nervous watching the Poles' religious fervour. However, the danger passed, and the delicate balance between Church and Party was maintained. The Poles coined a new slogan: 'Proletarians of all the lands, for the love of God unite!'

It was to be expected that the Polish sense of humour would take the opportunity of the great occasion of the papal visit for all kinds of jokes. In Party circles, said one story, they predicted that in a few years the Pope would come again to Warsaw with the words: 'Colonel Wojtila reporting back – mission accomplished.'

Since the Polish people understand their government's difficulties, jokes against it are more resigned than sarcastic. What really upsets the average Pole are food shortages, for they like to eat well – a trait that might have been stimulated by the traditional friendship with the French. 'What is fifty metres long and eats potatoes?' asks a jocular question. Answer: 'A queue outside a butcher's shop.' A customer asks his butcher first for pork, then for lamb, and lastly for beef. No luck. When he leaves, the butcher says to his assistant, 'What a fantastic memory!' A man in a queue outside a butcher's shop gets furious: 'I've had enough of this standing and waiting. I'm going off to murder the Prime Minister.' Two hours later he returns, looking glum. 'No good,' he says. 'There was a queue.'

In order to prevent new riots over food prices, the Polish government subsidizes them heavily – to the tune of no less than 12 per cent of the budget. Taking Lenin's 'New Economic Policy' of the early 1920s as their model, the authorities set up special shops for selling otherwise unobtainable goods for dollars and other hard currencies, and also 'commercial' shops offering meat and sausages for zloties – but at much higher prices than the official ones. During the papal visit, a hypothetical question was being asked: What name would Party chief Eduard Gierek assume if he were elected Pope? The answer: Inno-cents Commercius.

Wisecracks about the Polish currency, the zloty, abound: 'What have America and Poland in common?' 'In neither country can you buy anything with zloties.' The Polish Minister of Finance is sacked, according to one joke. The US government invites him to become its budget director. Why? In America the value of the dollar has been falling; in Poland it is always rising. There is a popular explanation of the average Pole's personal budget: he earns 4,000 zloties a month, spends 7,000, and saves the rest.

Any visitor to Poland will confirm that the people hate the Germans, the Czechs and especially the Russians.

There is only one point in favour of the Soviet Union, say the Poles: it is such an effective buffer between Poland and China. One of the many sarcastic stories about the Russians tells of Brezhnev and Kosygin flying back from a visit to Poland's ruler Gomulka in the 1960s:
'Did you see the beautiful watch Comrade Gomulka was wearing?' Kosygin asks Brezhnev.
'No,' says Brezhnev, 'show it to me.'
That joke is, of course, a revival of the anti-Russian story of 1815 about the three soldiers.

Despite Gomulka's mistakes, which led to his dismissal after the violent riots of 1970 in the Baltic ports, he had been responsible for lifting a great many restrictions on people's civil and religious freedom. In fact, there seems to be no fear of denunciation or arrest when the Poles joke about political matters. Quips about Communism are circulating freely, for instance: 'Who invented Communism?' Answer: 'The politicians, of course. If Communism had been invented by the scientists, they would have tried it out on animals first.' Or: 'Capitalism is the exploitation of man by man; Communism is the reverse.'

One joke acknowledges Poland's freer atmosphere compared to its neighbours. Two dogs meet at the Czech–Polish frontier:
'I'm going to emigrate to your country,' says the Polish dog. 'I hear you can get meat in Czechoslovakia.'
'And I'm crossing to Poland,' says the Czech dog. 'I'm told that at least you can bark there.'

Some jokes seem to wander from one East European country to another. This one has been told with a Bucharest café but also with a Belgrade grocer's shop as its setting:
'I want some tea,' says a customer.
'Certainly, sir. Russian or Chinese?'
The customer hesitates before answering that question.
'On second thoughts, make it coffee,' he says at last.

The Yugoslavs have a satirical journal, *Yesh* (Hedgehog), which can take much greater liberties than Russia's *Crocodile*; however, readers can always tell when *Yesh* has gone too far – the editor is replaced. The widest scope for criticism is shown in the journal's critical cartoons; a typical one depicted a restaurant customer gobbling up his meal at top speed to beat the next price increase. For Yugoslavia, too, has its inflation.

The country is, of course, outside the Soviet orbit, but Roumania has also achieved a certain degree of independence from Moscow. A 'blue' Roumanian joke is the definition of perverse love. There are three main kinds: sodomy, pederasty and love of the Soviet Union. Domestic shortcomings due to the prevailing system are the subjects of many anecdotes. A popular one is the story about a newcomer who arrives in hell and sees, to his astonishment, an angel working at the tea kettles. 'How come he's here amongst us sinners?' asks the newcomer. 'That's a Roumanian angel,' he is told. 'He has found that one can't make a living on *one* salary alone; so he does a bit of moonlighting as a teaboy down here.'

In several satellite countries, this story was told about Mao's famous swim in the Yangtze. As he reaches the river bank, the onlookers duly cheer and congratulate him. 'Just a moment,' he says. 'What I want to know first is who pushed me in!'

No jokes have come from Bulgaria, perhaps because the risk to the teller in this last outpost of Stalinism is too great. In 1963, a new law was enacted making it an offence to tell political jokes; its first victim, said the Bulgarian news agency, was an architect who got five years' imprisonment. Unfortunately, we do not know what story he had been telling.

'Why do we love the Soviet people?' asks a teacher in the German Democratic Republic.

Little Fritz lifts his arm: 'Because they liberated us.'

'And why do we hate the Americans?'

'Because they didn't liberate us,' answers little Hans.

The people in that eastern part of Germany have been out of luck: Hitler's dictatorship gave way directly to Russian control, without any breathing-space in between. The Soviets saw to it that the GDR regime was fashioned strictly after the Stalinist model. No wonder the people's political humour took over much of the pattern of the anti-Nazi jokes, bringing them up to date to fit the post-war situation. Still, there are also plenty of new quips and stories lampooning their Russian-style bureaucracy with its inefficiency and its repression of democracy which, alas, appears only in the country's official name, not much in the daily life of its citizens. Only once did the people try to impose their will on the 'democratic' authorities when, in 1953, the workers of East Berlin and other towns rebelled against certain new regulations. Soviet tanks restored order.

At that time there was a sarcastic story about a group of 'Young Communists' being taken to a parade of garlanded Soviet tanks. The German lads converse with the Soviet soldiers in Russian, which they have learned at school.

'Do you always drive around with these flowers?' asks a boy.

'No,' replies the soldier, 'they are only for demonstration.'

'And these,' asks the boy, pointing to the machine-gun barrels, 'what are they for?'

'They are against demonstration,' replies the Russian.

A similar story is still being told about the People's Police, called Vopo. An elderly lady meets a senior police officer at a social gathering and asks him in what campaign he earned the medal he is wearing.

'That's a Socialist award,' he says, 'and I got it for my services in peacetime.'

'I see,' says the old lady. 'I quite forgot that the Vopo also shoot at civilians.'

In order to keep the East Germans in East Germany, the regime built a wall along its frontiers with West Germany.

'What would you do,' a GDR soldier asks his mate as they are guarding the Berlin section of the wall, 'if this thing were suddenly pulled down?'

'I'd climb up the nearest tree.'

'But why?'

'I don't want to be trampled down by the crowd!'

Yet it would be wrong to assume that all the East Germans would prefer to live in prosperous West Germany. Again emulating the Russian example, the GDR has expelled some of its most irksome critics, mainly writers and other intellectuals who had no intention of leaving but who regarded it as their moral and political duty to stay on and speak out. The greatest mistake of this kind on the part of the East German rulers was the 'sneak' expulsion of Wolf Biermann, the highly popular singer and composer of satirical songs, in 1976 – he had been allowed to tour West Germany and then was deprived of his GDR citizenship while absent so that he was unable to return. Other critics of the regime, such as the leading novelist of East Germany, Stefan Heym, were banned from publishing their works at home and then prosecuted for 'breaking the currency laws' when they published them in the West. Thus any criticism of conditions in the GDR finds its expression only in whispered jokes, just as under Hitler.

A sophisticated 'register of the best traditions of the GDR' lists them as being rooted in mankind's history: the production methods in primeval society; human relations in the age of slavery; the class structure in feudal society; and the contradictions of the whole system in capitalism. One wisecrack traces the 'free' elections in the GDR back to Adam and Eve: God created her from Adam's rib and told him, 'Now choose a wife for yourself!'

A slight modification of the Bible features in the story of a group of dead GDR citizens who discover that hell, too, is divided into an eastern and a western sector. Given the choice, those who believe themselves to be ideologically sound opt for the eastern hell. A fact-finding delegation arrives from the western hell; they complain:

'Conditions on our western side are terrible; we've been boiled in oil three times already and roasted half a dozen times. How are things with you, in the eastern hell?'

'Fine,' is the answer. 'They've run out of fuel.'

Some leading economists from East Germany have been invited to Africa to modernize the Sahara area. Nothing changes in the first year, nothing in the second. In the third year the Sahara runs out of sand.

Socialist education, GDR style, comes in for a good deal of humorous criticism. A comrade sends his wife on a cooking course. After six months she comes home on leave and cooks a meal for her husband. He is furious:

'You haven't learnt a thing! The meat is burnt to cinders!'

'So sorry,' she sobs, 'but in our course we've only got as far as the Russian October Revolution.'

A few popular jokes deal with sexual problems. A husband comes home and finds his wife in bed with a lover. He reprimands her: 'Here you are canoodling, and they've got lemons at the State shop today!'

Ulbricht, who was appointed Head of State in 1960, was certainly not a man to everybody's taste. A story tells of the one remaining passenger in the last tramcar heading for the outskirts of East Berlin. He asks the conductor, 'Just as a matter of interest, how do you feel about Ulbricht?' The conductor looks over his shoulder to the driver and says to the passenger, 'Stay on to the terminal, and I'll tell you.' At the final stop, he motions the passenger to follow him and takes him to a wood. When they are out of everybody's earshot, the conductor whispers, 'You want to know what I feel about Ulbricht? Well, I like him.'

The Russian tanks that drove up against the East Berlin

workers in 1953 had already been stationed near the
town, ready for eventualities. Three years later, the
Russian tanks that were rushed to Budapest came from
the Hungarian provinces where they had been positioned
– just in case. The occasion was a rebellion in the capital
which had begun with a students' demonstration in
support of democratic elections, freedom of speech, and
a relaxation of the country's laws. The rebellion ended
with 2,700 dead, with show trials, executions and long-
term prison sentences. The Soviet leaders had stopped the
secession of Hungary from the Eastern bloc; Hungary
was back in the fold.

Since those tragic days, the Hungarians have managed
to win back some of their liberties and to turn their
political system into what they like to call, after their
favourite national dish, 'goulash Communism'. One
story they tell concerns a meeting between a Hungarian
and an East German worker. 'I have a good job,' says the
latter, 'a nice flat and a Wartburg car – I can't complain.'
The Hungarian retorts, 'I have all these things too; but I
can complain.' If the Hungarians have reason to do so,
they do it with their traditional good humour: 'We
are the jolliest barracks in the eastern concentration
camp.'

In 1977, a Budapest professor of ethnography, Imre
Cotona, published some of the 3,000 political jokes he
had collected over a period of thirty years. Many of them
are, from the point of view of the Party, rather near the
knuckle; for instance: 'How did the two German states
divide the heritage of Karl Marx between them?' 'The
German Democratic Republic has the Manifesto, the
Federal Republic has the Capital.' Or: 'Why did the
Hungarian government send a delegation of economists
to Australia?' 'To find out from the kangeroos how to do
a big leap with an empty pouch.' Another joke recorded
by Professor Cotona is this conversation between two
Hungarians: 'It's disgusting how our workers are
standing around instead of working.' 'Why does that
surprise you? The ruling class has never been working in

Hungary.' It seems that the dark days of 1956 have been all but forgotten, only the mistrust of Russia remains.

In 1968, it was Czechoslovakia's turn, but this time the men in the Kremlin did not have any Soviet tanks or troops at their disposal in the recalcitrant country itself; a full-scale invasion, with the participation of five states – the Soviet Union, Poland, Hungary, East Germany and Bulgaria – was organized. Their forces entered Czechoslovakia and converged on Prague.

The country had had a dramatic history. The ancient kingdom of Bohemia, with neighbouring Moravia and Slovakia, had been annexed into the Habsburg Empire at the beginning of the Thirty Years' War. With the defeat of Austria at the end of the First World War, these lands were at last released from three centuries of occupation. The victorious powers, America, Britain and France, helped to shape the new Czechoslovakia into a modern democracy. Yet only two decades later, the leaders of Britain and France handed it over on a platter to Hitler in the hope of appeasing him and saving Europe from another war. For six years Czechoslovakia was a German 'protectorate', until the Soviet army marched in and drove the Germans out. For the next three years, Czechoslovakia seemed well on its way to becoming a democracy again, with a moderate Socialist structure. Then, in 1948, a Communist coup turned it away from the West and affiliated it to the Soviet Union as one of her new satellites. However, despite their gratitude to the Russians for liberating them in the War, what happened in 1968 was not how the Czechs had envisaged their future.

A new leader with new ideas had emerged in the autumn of 1967, the Slovak Alexander Dubček. He found enthusiastic support among the people, and used his position as the Secretary-General of the Communist Party to start a reform movement which the Czechs dubbed the 'Prague spring'. It was to realize more or less what the students of Budapest had demanded: political and personal freedom as the citizens of western Europe

enjoyed it, though based on the original ideas of
Socialism. Dubček called it 'Socialism with a human face'.
The Kremlin men grew alarmed.

It all ended like the Hungarian rebellion. Soviet tanks –
the troops of the other satellite states were no more than
token forces – rolled into Prague. But the Czechs were
not frightened: they were mad with anger, and they
turned the Russian soldiers' trip 'in support of a fraternal
Socialist neighbour' into a nightmare journey. First, as
the tanks moved into position on the central Wenceslas
Square, there was not a soul in sight; the comradely
welcome the Russians had expected just did not happen.
'It was a haunting spectacle,' reported a British journalist.
'Down the right-hand pavement of the immense
boulevard the heavy Soviet tanks stood in isolation. The
population of Prague was showing its contempt for
them.'

Then the people began to drift back. Many brought
bricks and stones with them which they hurled at the
tanks, shouting and jeering. Some demonstrators had
crayons with which they scrawled slogans and signs
on the invaders' vehicles: 'Brezhnev = Hitler', 'Lenin –
wake up! Brezhnev has gone mad'; a number of tanks
were daubed with the jagged SS sign of Hitler's crack
regiments. 'This is a picture which will always stay in my
mind,' wrote the British correspondent. 'A blonde
Prague girl crawling under the fixed bayonets of a tank
crew, standing up and chalking a swastika on the
monster's bows. Then she spat, and crawled back again.
The soldiers looked on helplessly. In their faces was
written bewilderment and shame … Nothing is more
painful for Russian soldiers than to be compared to
Fascists.'

As the second day of the Soviet occupation dawned, the
spirit of Shveyk, the Czech master of sly insubordination,
seemed to have gripped the city. An entirely new
resistance campaign began, fought with brush and paint,
paper and cardboard – and with Czech wit, the people's
main defence against brute force. Hundreds of posters

appeared on the walls and hoardings, most of them in Russian: 'Ivan, go home, Olga is in bed with Igor', 'We are in mourning, some Russians have already committed suicide', 'Moscow return journey: only 1,800 kilometres'. A poster put up on a Czech car mangled by a Soviet tank said, 'A monument to Soviet culture'. 'Since you are here, why don't you just die of hunger?' asked one poster. Another was a mock telegram from a Prague maternity clinic to Brezhnev: 'Twelve counter-revolutionaries born here today. Send more tanks immediately.'

At least two posters, with cartoons, retold the fairy-tale of Little Red Riding Hood. 'What great eyes you've got, grandma,' she says to the big bad Russian wolf. 'Big eyes hell,' growls the wolf, 'I can't even see well enough to find my way home.' On the other poster, Red Riding Hood asks the wolf: 'Why have you got such big teeth?' and he replies, 'So that when I've eaten up my rations I can eat up all you children.'

The Russians got busy tearing the posters down, but for every one removed two new ones appeared. It was the voice of the people, addressed – under these tragic and exceptional circumstances – directly to the enemy. From all accounts, the effects were just what the Czechs wanted: to make it clear to these young Russian soldiers that they had been misled, that their leaders had sent them not on a mission of aid but of oppression, that they were hated intruders. To rub the message in, the words *'Russki idete domoi'*, 'Russians go home', frowned at them from the walls. What would they tell the folks at home?

But brute force and a show of strength were not the only trials the Czechs had to suffer. Soviet secret police turned up in black Volga cars with lists, drawn up by Czech quislings, of people suspected of actively supporting Dubček's 'Socialism with a human face'. Within a few hours of the first arrests and raids, the Prague citizens reacted in a most Shveyk-like fashion. 'I got the fright of my life,' reported an American who happened to be staying with relatives, 'when I heard a scratching sound at the door. I opened it quickly, and there was a kid – no more than fourteen – unscrewing the house number. He said that he was just making things difficult for the police.'

Thousands of house numbers must have been unscrewed that night, as well as hundreds of street signs. They were replaced by makeshift boards saying 'Dubček Street', 'Černik Street' or 'Svoboda Street', the latter two being the names of members of Dubček's government; 'Svoboda' appeared particularly often because the name also means 'freedom'.

'The Czechs are playing hell,' a British visitor wrote home. 'They switch names – and suddenly the secret police arrive, like something out of a gangster film. All chaos breaks out when the find they're in the wrong street. I saw one lot quarrelling furiously. They just couldn't agree whether the street name was wrong or they were.'

On many streets, notices revealed the names of local collaborators or police spies. Effigies of known quislings were set up in one of Prague's parks. Some posters listed the registration numbers of cars used by the secret police.

'The Patriot's Ten Commandments' was the title of a leaflet which seemed to be in everybody's hands after a few days of occupation. It said:

(1) We know nothing.
(2) We haven't heard anything.
(3) We have nothing.
(4) We give nothing.
(5) We cannot do anything.
(6) We understand nothing.
(7) We sell nothing.
(8) We cannot help.
(9) We reveal nothing.
(10) We won't forget anything.

As after the Hungarian rebellion and occupation, the outcome was a puppet government in Prague. Dubček was expelled from the Party and demoted to some humiliating job in his native Slovakia. There was a general purge of Party members, and a tightening of censorship of the press and the other media. The next Christmas number of the popular magazine *Reporter*, which had been banned by the Russians but suddenly appeared again on the news-stands, carried a cartoon on its front page. It showed the Holy Family; looking fondly but anxiously into the cradle, Mary says to Joseph, 'He'll have a hard life. He's got a human face.'

Moscow installed an obedient hardliner, Gustav Husak, as the new leader in Prague; inevitably, his subservience to the Russians was the subject of a number of Czech jokes. Husak, said one, telephones the Kremlin; Brezhnev takes the call, with Kosygin listening as Brezhnev speaks:

'No, no, no, no, yes ...'

'Leonid,' asks Kosygin, 'why did you say yes to Husak?'

'He asked me if he could hang up now.'

The effect of the Soviet invasion was that for the following decade Czech underground jokes were predominantly anti-Russian: this was clearly the most powerful feeling among the people. While the invasion troops were still present, this Shveykish story was being told:

A citizen goes to his local police station and reports, 'A Swiss soldier has stolen my Russian watch.'

The policeman looks at him sternly.

'Pull yourself together and make a sensible report,' he says. 'A Swiss soldier stealing a Russian watch? Surely you mean a Russian soldier has stolen your Swiss watch!'

'You said it, not me,' grins the citizen.

The good Fairy Wishfulfilment stops three Czechs in the woods and asks them what they would like to come true:

'I wish that on Monday the Chinese army would march into Prague, stay for a day, and then march back again,' says the first Czech.

'I wish that the Chinese army would march into

Prague on Wednesday, stay for the day, and then march
home,' says the second Czech.

The fairy is rather puzzled, but carries on listening to
the third man who has exactly the same wish, only that it
should happen on Friday. The fairy promises to do her
best, but asks why they all want the same thing, only on
different days.

'Well,' they tell her, 'who could wish for more than the
Chinese army marching through the Soviet Union half a
dozen times in one week?'

Again, as in the days before the short 'Prague spring',
one had to look over one's shoulder to make sure there
were no unwelcome listeners, and strangers had to be
treated with caution. One story told of a citizen reading a
motoring magazine in a Prague café. Another man sits
down next to him and notices that the reader is studying
the pictures of a Rolls-Royce and a Russian Moskvitch
car.

'I wonder which of them you'd like to have,' says the
newcomer.

The man looks up and replies, 'The Moskvitch, of
course.'

'Come, come, you obviously know nothing about
cars!'

'Oh yes,' says the reader. 'I know a lot about cars. But I
know nothing about you.'

After the 1968 purge of Dubček's sympathizers, two
bears meet in the Carpathian mountains, a Czech and a
Russian one. They swap sob stories about their hard lives.
'Since the working norms for dancing bears were raised,'
says the Russian bear, 'I have to work so much that in the
evening I fall into my lair completely exhausted.' The
Czech bear sighs, 'I wish I were allowed to dance at all.
But since they struck me off the list of the Performing
Bears' Union, I have to make my living in the Bohemian
forest as a cuckoo.'

Cyril and Methodius were ninth-century saints; born
in Thessalonica, they were said to have designed the
Slavonic ('Cyrillic') alphabet. They taught the Christian

faith first to the Bulgarians and later to the people of Moravia, where Methodius was appointed Archbishop. Tradition has it that both saints were buried somewhere in Moravia, and archaeological research in our time has been going on to discover their graves. One of them was found – so the story goes – and a team of Russian scientists was brought in to join the Czechoslovak archaeologists and solve the question whether the skeleton in the grave was the remains of St Cyril or St Methodius.

The Russians went to work on the problem. Some time later they brought the remains to Prague in a bundle tied with a string. The skull of the skeleton had been fractured, the spine broken, the fingers shattered.

'It's Cyril,' the Russians declared to their Czechoslovak colleagues.

'But how do you know?' the Russians were asked.

'The saint confessed it himself.'

'After having been buried for a thousand years?'

'Ah well, we have our ways of making people talk,' explained the Russians.

Oddly enough, this story was broadcast, in a different version, in 1969 by the German-language programme of Radio Warsaw. However, it was no longer a skeleton from Moravia identified by Russian scientists – it was a mummy from an ancient Egyptian tomb, and the Greek dictator Papadopoulos had come with a team of archaeologists from Athens to identify it for the Egyptian ruler Nasser. They informed him of their findings: it was the mummy of some pharaoh. Nasser: 'How do you know?' 'He told us so himself,' and the story had the same pay-off as the Moravian one. Some Polish humorist had adapted it as a joke against the Greek dictatorship.

The Greeks themselves had, of course, their own sarcastic stories about the Colonels' regime while it lasted. Papadopoulos, said one joke, visits Chairman Mao in Peking:

'How many dissidents do you reckon you have in your country?' he asks him.

'A very small number,' replies Mao, 'no more than eight or nine million.'

'Hm, about the same as us,' says the Greek ruler.

Brigadier Patakos and his wife are going to celebrate their wedding anniversary. He promises to give her any present she would like.

'What I'd like best,' she says, 'would be that you open the frontiers of our country.'

'I knew it, sweetheart,' says Patakos. 'You want us to be alone.'

Both Papadopoulos and Patakos were arrested when their regime collapsed. In their heyday they had made a great show of personally investigating complaints about conditions in Greece. The headmaster of a school grumbles about overcrowding, bad lighting and lack of teachers.

'Sorry,' says Papadopoulos, 'the State has no money for improvements.'

The next visit takes the two rulers to a prison, where they listen to the inmates' complaints.

'Bad food?' says Papa Dop. 'You'll get a new cook and steaks every day. Bored? I'll have television sets installed in all the cells.'

Patakos is baffled: 'Why do you do nothing for the school and yet so much for the prison?'

'My dear Stelio,' answers Papa Dop, 'We'll never have to go back to school.'

Then there was a corny joke, surely not told in Greece for the first time, about the foreign tourist who hails a taxi in Athens, asking the driver, 'Are you free?' – and the driver mutters his answer, 'Alas, sir, I am a Greek.'

After nearly half a century of dictatorship under Salazar and his successor Caetano, the Portuguese got busy purging the country's public and industrial life of Fascists. This story satirized the purge: The manager of a Lisbon factory was called before the workers' committee and severely criticized for the autocratic way in which he had ruled the place. However, it would have been unwise to sack him since experienced managers were rare. So it was decided to give him a chance to redeem himself: he was to stand a whole day in the Avenida da Liberdade, the capital's main thoroughfare, with a placard around his neck saying, 'I was a Fascist'. Then all would be forgiven.

The morning after his day of penance the manager reported back at the factory. He was in a rather bad state; his ribs were black and blue. 'What happened?' he was asked. 'Were you beaten up?'

'Oh no. But people kept creeping up to me, digging me in the ribs with their elbows, pointing to my placard and whispering, "So was I." '

'Freedom begets wit, and wit begets freedom,' wrote Jean Paul, the popular German humorist of the early nineteenth century. That was certainly true at that time and in a country ruled by dozens of kings, dukes and little princes, each of them anxious to stifle criticism and opposition. But is it still true in a modern democracy? Freedom of expression does not produce, or indeed need wit as a weapon where the government is freely elected; for if the majority of the people feel that it ought to be changed they can vote it out of power. Political humour has its legitimate outlet in the media. This is the reason why popular satire has declined in the democracies of the West and whispered jokes have no function to fulfil.

Thus satire has been rarer in England than in other countries, and fewer political jokes have been recorded. It is almost as though satire has been regarded as an un-British activity, at least in modern times. Humour has always been an essential part of the life of the nation, but its purpose is rather to amuse than to attack. Satire, on the other hand, is militant, and there have been few periods in English history when attacks by words (and pictures) were the only means of fighting an oppressive establishment. Bernard Shaw was once called 'a demolition expert with a genius for intellectual slum-clearance, not for town-planning', and his satire was often felt to be negative. Perhaps the average Englishman does not like to be aroused from his comfortable easy chair to face uncomfortable facts, and still less to be asked to do something about them.

A valiant attempt to revive satire was made in Britain in the early 1960s with a few cabaret-type revues in the theatre and particularly with the television series 'That Was The Week That Was', which was very witty and highly entertaining but was stopped after some months when it began to run out of targets to attack. At about the same time, the country got its new satirical journal, *Private Eye*, which has never run out of targets since it extended its range to zones conventionally regarded as sacrosanct, such as Buckingham Palace. For instance, in one of its famous montages – press photographs with typed-in speech 'bubbles' – the Duke of Edinburgh was made to reply to the question why he married the Queen: 'Because she was there.' Once, Scotland Yard got a mock ad for its recruiting campaign with the motto, 'It's a real thug's life in the New Police Force!'

Generally, it is the powerful, the rich, and the famous who receive *Private Eye's* special attention; the bumbling, hypocritical, pompous politicians and others in the public limelight are lampooned, with the result that the journal has found itself in one libel suit after another – while its circulation has risen to six figures. This is a long way from its origins in some university, from where came also the casts of the satirical revues of the period. Richard Ingrams, the founder and still the editor-in-charge, had just left college when he started the journal with a few fellow-students in 1961, and there was much schoolboy humour in the early issues. But soon *Private Eye* grew up to become a true descendant of the satirists of the early nineteenth century, and to some extent also a British counterpart to France's *Canard Enchaîné*, particularly with its daring revelations of 'swineries in public life', its 'savage sanity amid the rattle of skeletons being hastily thrust back into closets', as *The Times* columnist Bernard Levin put it.

Admittedly, *Private Eye* is so popular because it is, first and foremost, jolly good entertainment. British democracy would probably survive without it; so does democracy in the USA, where there is no equivalent satirical publication. Will Rogers, America's leading humorist in the early days of radio, once said it was almost too easy to be a comic when you had the whole administration as unintentional collaborators; he would have been sorry to see them go, so why should he campaign for a better government with his jokes?

However, those nations which really need a better government also need their whispered jokes. How badly they need them can always be gauged by the number of satirical stories taken over from the past or from another country, and adapted to fit the prevailing circumstances.

Thus we meet that old retainer from the Kremlin wall again in the Czechoslovakia of the 1970s. Ivan has become Jan, and instead of a trumpet he has a telescope. A visiting American senator sees him perched on a hilltop, peering through his instrument:

'What are you doing?' asks the American.

'I'm employed by the Party to scan the horizon for the dawn of the Age of Socialist Plenty,' says Jan.

The senator, worried about the state of the economy in his own country, asks him whether he would be able to apply his talents to giving an early warning of the collapse of capitalism.

'Of course,' replies the Czech.

'Then I might be able to get you a job in New York. You could sit at the top of the Empire State Building with your telescope. Would fifty thousand dollars a year be enough?'

Jan thinks this over, but refuses.

'Why?' asks the senator.

'Because here,' says Jan, 'I have a job for life. But if I accept your offer I might be out of work in a year or two.'

Bibliography

Appignanesi, Lisa. *The Cabaret*. London, 1975
Ashton, John. *Humour, Wit, and Satire of the Seventeenth Century*. London, 1883
Bergson, Henri. *Le Rire*. Paris, 1900
Brandt, H. J. *Witz mit Gewähr*. Stuttgart, 1965
Fodor, Laszlo & Richardson, Vivian. *Axis to Grind*. New York, 1943
Freud, Sigmund. Standard edition vols VIII & XXI. London, 1960
Gotfurt, Dorothea (trsl.). '*While I'm Sitting on the Fence*', *Songs from the German*. London, 1967
Ingrams, Richard (Ed.). *The Life and Times of Private Eye*. London, 1971
Landmann, Salcia. *Der jüdische Witz*. Olten, 1960
Larsen, Egon. *Weimar Eyewitness*. London, 1976
Linfield, Eric G. & Larsen, Egon (Ed.). '*Laughter in a Damp Climate*', *700 years of British Humour*. London, 1963
Sutherland, James. *English Satire*. London, 1958
Wardroper, John. *Jest upon Jest*. London, 1970
Wardroper, John. *Kings, Lords, and Wicked Libellers*. London, 1973
Wendel, Friedrich. *Geschichte in Anekdoten*. Berlin, 1924.

The author wishes to express his thanks to Mr Eric G. Linfield for his valuable literary advice, and to Bavarian Radio, Munich, for permission to use some material from its foreign correspondents, broadcast in 1979.